The Psychology of Self and Other

The Psychology
of Self
and Other

ELIZABETH R. MOBERLY

TAVISTOCK PUBLICATIONS   London & New York

First published in 1985 by
Tavistock Publications Ltd
11 New Fetter Lane, London EC4P 4EE

Published in the USA by
Tavistock Publications
in association with Methuen, Inc.
733 Third Avenue, New York, NY 10017

Photoset by Rowland Phototypesetting Ltd
Bury St Edmunds, Suffolk
Printed in Great Britain at the
University Press, Cambridge

British Library
Cataloguing in Publication Data

Moberly, Elizabeth R.
The psychology of self and other.
1. Psychoanalysis
I. Title
616.89' 17   RC504

ISBN 0-422-79740-5

Library of Congress
Cataloging in Publication Data

Moberly, Elizabeth R.
The psychology of self and other.

Bibliography: p.
Includes indexes.
1. Self. 2. Ego (Psychology)
3. Transference (Psychology)   I. Title.
BF697.M566 1985   155.2   85-2657

ISBN 0-422-79740-5

Contents

Preface

The present study follows up the more general implications of my work on the early development of gender identity in *Psychogenesis* (Moberly 1983). Here the chief emphasis is on narcissistic and borderline psychopathology, with particular reference to the contributions of Heinz Kohut and Otto Kernberg. The functional psychoses also receive some comment, again developing the conclusions reached in *Psychogenesis*. I present a general review of basic Freudian concepts, and develop Bowlby's work on attachment and separation, as well as Kohut's data on selfobject transferences. On this basis, I offer a dynamic theory of developmental arrest: the repression of an attachment-need checks the process of intrapsychic structuralization; but the re-emergence of the repressed – in the form of a selfobject transference – implies an inherent reparative potential, through which the normal developmental process may be resumed and continued. However, as the selfobject transference implies the reanimation and reinstatement of legitimate developmental needs, it is vital that such needs should be fulfilled, and not merely acknowledged without gratification. The therapist's role as selfobject is seen as crucial – the only developmentally realistic therapeutic manoeuvre for disorders involving incomplete intrapsychic structuralization, viz. the functional psychoses, borderline states, and narcissistic personality disorders.

The concept of corrective emotional experience has from time to time been raised within psychoanalysis, but not as yet accepted. *The Psychology of Self and Other* argues that the body of *existing* psychoanalytic data itself logically demands the rehabilitation of this concept, understood as the normal developmental need for attachment to a selfobject. This is a work of theoretical revision with significant technical implications. Interpretation remains important for psychoanalytic technique, but it is to be divorced from the rule of abstinence, which is seen as counter-therapeutic for the whole spectrum of more serious disorders. The classical model for technique is to be revised in order to do justice to the implications of the analytic data. The data are not to be minimized or reduced in order to preserve unchanged a model that was originally shaped around more limited data. Corrective emotional experience – the fulfilment of legitimate developmental needs – is presented as an essential part of the therapeutic task. This study is offered as a challenge to psychoanalysis to accept the implications of its own data, and thereby to make advances in the treatment of the more serious forms of psychopathology.

I am grateful to the Leverhulme Trust for its award of a Fellowship for this work.

Elizabeth R. Moberly
Cambridge, 1982

1

Freudian concepts
reviewed

Bowlby's studies of mourning in early childhood (Bowlby,
Robertson, and Rosenbluth 1952; Bowlby *et al.* 1956; Bowlby
1960, 1961, 1963, 1973) comment on three phases of response to
the loss of a love-object: initial *protest*, which gives way to
subsequent *despair*, and finally leads to *detachment*. Detachment
is considered to be based on the repression of the child's need
for his mother (Bowlby *et al.* 1956). It is this attachment-need
which persists as a dynamic force in the unconscious. The
mourning-reaction set in train by separation may be resolved
sooner or later, and the ambivalence towards the love-object
(experienced as hurtful) may be adequately worked through.
However, I have suggested in *Psychogenesis* (Moberly 1983) that
in some instances pathological mourning-responses may never
be worked through. Repressed yearning for the loved object,
and repressed reproaches against it, may persist throughout
life. Most importantly, I see this as the origin of the paranoid
condition:

'The genesis of paranoia is seen to involve the formation, in a young child, of a defensive barrier against a love-source that is behaving hurtfully. In other words, the child represses his normal love-need, and the defensive barrier of mistrust and even hatred towards the hurtful love-source blocks the normal process of attachment to that love-source.'

(Moberly 1983: 15)

The same mechanism of defensive detachment – repression of an attachment-need – is seen as causative of both transsexualism and homosexuality. In both instances the normal process of receiving love from, and hence identifying with, a parental love-source of the same sex, has been blocked by trauma, especially in the earliest years of life. The resultant psychodynamic structure of both transsexualism and homosexuality is that of same-sex ambivalence – though the intensity of the defensive detachment and the corresponding extent of the unmet love-need vary considerably in degree in individual instances. It is indicated that the capacity for so-called 'homosexual' love actually marks the attempt to resume the normal developmental process, and thereby to fulfil hitherto unmet needs for same-sex love and identification. I conclude that the defensive manoeuvre involved was not against homosexual impulses *as such*: 'The fundamental defence, in each case, is against the same-sex love-source, which has resulted in the *normal* need for love from the parent of the same sex remaining unmet' (Moberly 1983: 28). The more general implications of such conclusions for psychoanalytic psychology will here be explored, commencing with the concept of defence.

Defence is a central concept in the history of psychoanalytic thought, and one of the earliest to be formulated. Freud (1896) took a crucial step beyond his contemporaries in seeing defence as pivotal for the development of psychological disorder: 'Defence [is] the nuclear point in the psychical mechanism of the neuroses in question.'[1]

Unfortunately, Freud's own formulations, and those of subsequent psychoanalytic thought, would seem to have misinterpreted the orientation of the concept of defence. Freud repeatedly insists that defence is directed against instinctual impulses.[2] He speaks of defence against an instinctual impulse which is 'unwelcome',[3] 'objectionable',[4] 'undesirable',[5] or 'dangerous'.[6] More recently, Laplanche and Pontalis have reaffirmed this interpretation: 'The two poles of the conflict are invariably the ego and the instinct: it is against an internal threat that the ego seeks to defend itself' (Laplanche and Pontalis 1980: 105). This seems illogical. To return to Bowlby's formulations, detachment takes place *vis-à-vis* the love-object that is experienced as hurtful. In other words, the defence is directed *against the love-object*, against a situation of external danger (separation, loss of the object). This defence against the love-object does involve the repression of the attachment-need. But it should be clear that this instinctual need is being *protected* against, or from, the hurtful love-object. The instinctual need is being defended; it is not being defended *against*. We may use the analogy of a shield. A shield is used for defence, but the person behind the shield is being defended from dangers beyond; he is not, himself, being defended against! Similarly, repression is a mechanism of defence, but what is repressed is what is *being* defended. The attachment-need is repressed in what is experienced as a situation of external danger. The need as such is in no way objectionable.

Though briefly stated, this point is of central importance, and suggests the need for a major reshaping of our theoretical perspectives. Outstandingly, it indicates that the resolution of defence or repression is by itself inadequate. The goal must be the actual restoration of attachment, in a relationship that will fulfil (gratify) those legitimate developmental needs that were left unmet when the attachment-need was repressed.

We may also reconsider the question posed by Freud[7] and re-echoed by Laplanche and Pontalis: 'How does it come about that instinctual discharge, which is given over by definition to the attainment of pleasure, can be perceived as unpleasure or as the threat of unpleasure to the point of occasioning a defensive operation?' (1980: 105–06). The perception is of external danger, not of internal unpleasure. The motivation is therefore the protection of the instinctual need. The suggestion of external danger has been mooted from the time of Freud onwards, but has been treated as peripheral. It has not hitherto affected the central formulation of the ego's defensive struggle against *instinctual* dangers. But with our proposed change of perspective, the question mentioned above would become redundant.

The significance of repression is in turn modified. Freud speaks of repression as analogous to flight,[8] as something between flight and condemnation,[9] to be replaced ultimately by a condemning judgment.[10] It is 'only a forerunner of the later-developed normal condemning judgment'.[11] This again misinterprets the orientation of repression, and ignores its protective function. *Protection* does not need to be replaced by condemnation, as the classical formulations unfortunately suggest. It is not the repressed (shielded) need that is objectionable, but the unavailability of the love-object. It is the love-object that is, as it were, 'condemned' for its hurtfulness, and it is precisely on this account that repression of the attachment-need takes place. Repression should be replaced, not by a 'condemning judgment', but by a restored attachment.

Repression is analogous to flight, but it still marks a flight from an external danger, not an internal one. The traditional distinction between internal and external dangers is certainly important. It is on this basis that we point out that repression involves the protection (withholding) of an internal need in the face of an external danger. The ego does not 'treat the instinctual danger as if it was an external one'.[12] The danger is actually external.

It may be noted in parenthesis that the repression of an unpleasant memory or idea can and does occur. But the repression of an instinctual need – the need for attachment – is quite another matter, and does not imply a negative evaluation of what is repressed. However, although the vicissitudes of instinctual needs are of crucial importance for psychological development, their repression has hitherto been evaluated in exactly the same terms as the repression of unpleasant memories. It is here argued that this equation of the two has been entirely misleading.

The issue involved in our discussion of repression is not instinctual *danger*, but instinctual *unfulfilment*. The love-object is perceived as hurtful, and for this reason the normal attachment-need to that object is held back (repressed). The overall goal must therefore be the restoration of attachment, and the undoing of repression must be regarded as only a means to this end, not as an end in itself. Since repression does not affect what is in conflict with the *ego*, we must be cautious in speaking of paving the way for reconciliation with the repressed material.[13] The elimination of repression is and must be a significant step. However, it is misleading to say that this takes place so that 'the libido cannot withdraw once more *from the ego* by flight into the unconscious'.[14] The ego required the libido to withdraw *from the object*. The undoing of repression, in the absence of a restored attachment to the object, would therefore not resolve the problem, merely provide a greater awareness of it.

In the light of this, we must insist that classical formulations of the nature of the therapeutic effect are unsatisfactory. To make conscious what is repressed in the id[15] may be a first step, but it is no more than that, when a repressed attachment-need is involved. We are not merely to educate the ego 'to overcome its inclination towards attempts at flight and to tolerate an approach to what is repressed'.[16] Such a statement mislocates the focus of conflict, since the flight was by the instinctual impulse from the unsatisfactory *object*. Likewise, the resolution of conflict is in itself inadequate. The objective must be to resume and continue what the conflict originally hindered, viz. the fulfilment of an attachment-need.

Historically, psychoanalysis distinguished itself from catharsis in the nature of its task: no longer to abreact affect, but to uncover repressions, and replace them by acts of judgment.[17] This formulation was valid in the early stages of analysis, which was concerned with the repression of painful ideations; but it was not valid to generalize from ideations to attachment-needs. *Only* in the case of painful ideations should repressions be replaced by acts of judgment. Attachment-needs, once freed from their protective repression, should be fulfilled through the medium of a restored attachment – and indeed, by their very nature, such needs cannot be fulfilled in any other way.

Repression checks the fulfilment of an attachment-need. It does not stop that need from existing in the unconscious.[18] Indeed, since the instincts are 'continuous in their nature',[19] repression is not merely an event that occurs once, but requires permanent expenditure of energy.[20] The repressed instinct 'never ceases to strive for complete satisfaction'.[21] However, it is unsatisfactory to equate this striving with the 'repetition of a primary experience of satisfaction'.[22] The reinstatement of an attachment-need would involve the *continuation* of what was originally checked. Fulfilling something as yet unmet is more than just repetition, and more purposive. Strictly speaking, it is not repetition at all, since it involves precisely what has not yet been attained.

At this point, the discussion has impinged on Freud's concept of a repetition-compulsion. The patient 'is obliged to *repeat* the repressed material as a contemporary experience instead of . . . *remembering* it as something belonging to the past'.[23] This compulsion to repeat 'must be ascribed to the unconscious repressed'.[24] We may entirely agree with the latter explanation, but will rewrite its implications in the light of what has been said already. Our data have suggested that the 'compulsion' is to fulfil and complete, to renew and continue what was checked earlier. In this sense, the compulsion is no more than the persistence of the need and its continued striving for satisfaction. Its compulsive character may be taken to suggest that the fulfilment of such a need is essential for normal human development and can only be ignored or left unfulfilled at the peril of such development. Precisely because the need has persisted unmet in the unconscious, the patient is obliged to *resume* the fulfilment of the repressed as a contemporary experience (to paraphrase Freud's statement), since the persistence of the unmet need is a genuinely contemporary fact.

To reiterate, the fulfilment of the need was originally checked in the past, and the need has therefore persisted unmet into the present. This implies that there is no justification for contrasting repetition with 'remembering . . . as . . . belonging to the past'.[25] Where an attachment-need is concerned, it may be helpful for the patient to become aware that the fulfilment of the need was checked in the past. But what does this awareness do *of itself* towards fulfilling the unmet need? Its lack of fulfilment is a present reality – due originally to a past mishap – and only its renewed fulfilment can solve a problem of this nature. The compulsion to repeat does not *replace* an impulsion to remember,[26] since the goal is not remembering as such, but a renewed attachment. Conscious awareness may help in the promotion of this goal, but it must be made entirely clear that it is not itself this goal.

Where a (repressed) attachment-need is involved, the compulsion to repeat does not seem to be problematic, but is essentially the attempt to resume and continue the developmental process from the point at which it was hindered or broken off. However, it is clear that the repetition compulsion does also involve what is unpleasant or painful. This is not because 'it brings to light activities of repressed instinctual impulses'.[27] We have already indicated that the conflict is not between the ego and the id. But whatever was conflictual in the past (*vis-à-vis* the object), and was not resolved, may still persist and require resolution. In this respect, the repetition compulsion would seem to mark the attempt to undo, resolve, or master. It does not as such suggest an abrogation of the pleasure principle.

Moreover, in no sense does it suggest a sufficient grounding for Freud's theoretical construct of the death instinct. There is, to appearances, an 'urge . . . to restore an earlier state of things'.[28] However, this 'return' to an earlier state must be regarded as more apparent than real, if in fact that 'earlier state' has persisted unchanged during the course of time. The unfulfilled attachment-need, or unresolved conflict, is as much a present problem as a past problem. Freud characterizes the unconscious as timeless and indestructible.[29] We would speak of the persistence of the unfulfilled and the unresolved. The earlier state has not truly been 'reinstated'. Rather, it has been there all the time, and is now made manifest. This is neither 'inertia' nor 'conservatism' – the concepts classically linked with the death instinct. It is simply a statement of incomplete development, or of lack of resolution of conflict, or both together.

It is in this light that we may also reassess the concepts of regression and fixation, and suggest a new perspective on their significance. These concepts are frequently invoked in psychoanalysis, but it is acknowledged that they are primarily descriptive rather than explanatory (Laplanche and Pontalis 1980). In practice, however, they are assigned a significance which – I wish to suggest – is actually the reverse of their meaning. The term 'regression' itself begs the question by implying, linguistically, a *return*. Freud repeatedly speaks of regression in terms of a *return* to something earlier,[30] and regards it as a movement from present to past. Consider, however, our basic paradigm: if an attachment-need was repressed in early years and its further fulfilment was thereby checked, there was no progress made in this area of development in the first place. It is not a question of *re*gression, but of lack of *pro*gress. At the same time, since this initial check in progress is not global, its consequences may not become apparent or fully apparent until later on. But 'regression' (so-called) is more apparent than real. We may speak of it as the later manifestation of an initial lack of progress. It is vital for both theoretical understanding and clinical practice that this concept of developmental inhibition should not be contrasted with regression,[31] but seen as its essential meaning.

The clinical data undergirding the concepts of regression and fixation are not in dispute, only the conclusions to be drawn from these data. I here suggest that it is the early repression of an attachment-need that results in fixation – fixating the normal developmental process at whatever point it has reached at the time of repression. And, because the developmental process is thereby checked (fixation), no further progress is made in this area of development (the possibility of apparent 'regression'). Indeed, the two halves of this statement are in effect tautologous, since to check progress itself implies lack of further progress. I emphasize this tautology only because the concepts of fixation and regression have not been so clearly and intrinsically linked hitherto. Apparent regression *to* a fixation point is to be recast as revealing a lack of progress *from* an initial fixation point. Thus, when Freud states that 'the essence of mental disease lies in a return to earlier states of affective life and functioning',[32] I would suggest instead that absence of normal development is essential to many forms of psychopathology. This may be manifested in an apparent return to earlier states of functioning, but I wish to suggest that these earlier states were never genuinely outgrown and superseded in the first place, even if a superficial adjustment masked the difficulties until later. At the same time, the continuing expenditure of energy on repression implies the persistence of the original conflict (*vis-à-vis* the hurtful object), which may well become apparent in the current clinical picture. The therapeutic goal must be both to resolve the conflict – undo the repression – and, most importantly, to renew the formerly interrupted process of growth. Unless the need for growth-through-attachment is resumed, maintained, and fulfilled, the central problem – of interrupted development – must remain unresolved. The provision of a renewed attachment must – according to our paradigm – be central to the therapeutic process. The resolution of repression is significant only as a means to this end, and not otherwise.

If a fixation to particular objects persists throughout life,[33] this implies that the attachment-need *vis-à-vis* these particular objects was blocked and has not yet been fulfilled. To speak of this as 'psychical inertia' or 'sluggishness of the libido'[34] is quite unsatisfactory. A normal developmental need persists precisely because it has not yet been satisfied. Only when fulfilled can it be superseded. To suggest that the libido is 'unwilling to abandon its fixations',[35] or that its mobility is ended 'through its intense opposition to detachment'[36] is a serious misinterpretation. Again, the clinical data are not in dispute, only their evaluation. What these data suggest is that legitimate developmental needs cannot be bypassed. If it happens that their fulfilment is checked, the needs still persist. To criticize this persistence is to misunderstand the nature of psychological development, and results in misinterpreting the therapeutic endeavour. So-called 'resistance' to release from archaic attachments (Laplanche and Pontalis 1980: 162) is entirely proper. Indeed, it is not right to speak of this as resistance, since it marks the persistence of a legitimate need, whose fulfilment has hitherto been blocked. Only fulfilment can result in 're-lease' from the need. Either the need will be fulfilled, or it will persist unfulfilled and still requiring fulfilment. The 'tenacity' or 'adhesiveness' of the libido is no more than the acknowledgement of this fact.

This discussion also suggests a re-evaluation of the relation between fixation and repression. On this model, fixation is neither the basis of repression, still less the first stage of repression (Laplanche and Pontalis 1980). Instead, it is the consequence of repression, inasmuch as the repression of an attachment-need checks – fixates – the normal developmental process of growth that takes place through the medium of an attachment to a love-object. We would not, therefore, speak of 'fixations from which the ego had protected itself in the past by repressions'.[37] Rather, the ego protects its instinctual needs for attachment from a hurtful love-object, and effects this protection by repression, thereby resulting in fixation. The developmental process is checked in consequence of experiencing the object as hurtful (whether deliberately or unintentionally so).

On this understanding, there is no reason why symptoms should disappear when their unconscious determinants have been rendered conscious.[38] Interpretation may well transform the unconscious into the conscious, but this increase of awareness can be only auxiliary and not central to the therapeutic task. The problem has been stated as the persistence, unfulfilled, of legitimate developmental needs. The normal timetable for their fulfilment was checked when the child's attachment-need was protectively repressed from the hurtful love-object in early years. Thus, the developmental needs that are normally fulfilled through the medium of an attachment have persisted as yet unfulfilled. The removal of repression is helpful, but in itself is only a stage towards the larger goal of renewed attachment. Freud's therapeutic formulation was that 'the change which is decisive for a favourable outcome is the elimination of repression, so that the libido cannot withdraw once more from the ego by flight into the unconscious'.[39] However, the libido did not flee from the ego in the first place, but from the hurtful object, at the protective instigation of the inchoate ego. This distinction is crucial, since it indicates that restoration of the libido to the object, rather than to the ego, must be the goal of the therapeutic endeavour. Thus, interpretation may enlarge the ego[40] in its cognitive sphere, but this is peripheral to the problem as stated. The inability or reluctance to reformulate the significance of repression has thus seriously hampered the scope of psychoanalysis. The model pertaining to the repression of painful ideations was correct, but of limited significance. The repression of attachment-needs is a different kind of problem, and calls for a corresponding re-evaluation of the goal and methods of therapy.

The data considered in this discussion point to the conclusion that the 'rule of abstinence' is of only limited value in the therapeutic endeavour; indeed it must often be contraindicated. The refusal to gratify the analysand's libidinal demands is designed to ensure 'that the patient finds as few substitutive satisfactions for his symptoms as possible' (Laplanche and Pontalis 1980: 2). The economic justification for the rule of abstinence is to ensure that the libido released by treatment is 'not immediately redirected towards a fresh cathexis of external objects . . . [but is] transferred into the analytic situation' (Laplanche and Pontalis 1980: 3). However, where the problem is an unfulfilled attachment-need, it is precisely the 'fresh cathexis of external objects' that is and must be the solution to the problem. This need can be met within the analytic situation. Indeed, if it is not met within the analytic situation, this implies nothing less than the abdication of psychoanalysis from the treatment of any problem that involves more than merely the repression of painful ideations. It must be stressed that it is the nature of the problem that must shape the nature of the solution. The classical model of psychoanalysis fits one kind of problem, but does not do justice to more complex forms of pathology, on the data that psychoanalysis itself has provided. The classical model may not rightly be regarded as normative for all aspects of analytic work.

An interchange based on verbal expression by the patient and interpretation by the analyst is helpful but insufficient, *where legitimate developmental needs still require to be fulfilled.* Freud's direction to the analyst was neither to gratify, nor to suppress, the patient's craving for love.[41] This rule is valuable in a limited sphere. Our postulate is that the removal of repression must in many instances be complemented by 'gratification' – or, better, developmental fulfilment. Repression in itself is not the problem, but only a hindrance to the solution of the problem. Even when repression is resolved, the problem as such still remains, viz. the lack of fulfilment of attachment-needs. Transference love is not to be treated as unreal[42] if it involves the re-emergence of legitimate developmental needs. It may be unusual for such needs to persist unmet into adult life, but the needs are still as real as they were in earlier years. If their phase-specific fulfilment was checked, the therapeutic task must be to resume the fulfilment of the developmental time-table.

This is not to advocate a 'cure by love' in preference to a 'cure by analysis',[43] but to widen the scope of the analytic endeavour. 'Control over instinct'[44] will remain part of the analytic task. At the same time, it must often be regarded as counter-therapeutic to deny the patient 'precisely those satisfactions which he desires most intensely and expresses most importunately'.[45] Instinctual privation has traditionally been regarded as essential to motivate the patient to work towards change.[46] For the reasons already given, this may not rightly be regarded as a general rule. The patient's repetitive behaviour is not necessarily a hindrance to the work of recollection, but is often a valid attempt towards the goal of meeting unfulfilled developmental needs.

The concept of transference implies 'what is transferred'. Freud speaks of 'new editions or facsimiles';[47] the replacement of an earlier person by the analyst;[48] the past applied to the present;[49] 'new impressions or reprints'.[50] I wish to add to this the possibility of transferring – and thereby resuming – unfulfilled developmental needs. If an attachment-need emerges from repression, it may well be transferred to the person of the analyst. The conscious awareness of this fact does nothing to remove or destroy the transference,[51] nor should it do so. To 'remove' the transference of this unfulfilled need would be to reinstate the very problem that requires solution.

What is transferred may include negative attitudes originally directed towards a parent, and it is right that these should be resolved. Where unmet needs are transferred, it is right that these should be fulfilled. Transference can involve both repetition (of infantile reactions) *and* reinstatement (of unmet developmental needs). Freud's constant insistence on repetition in the transference[52] covers only one side of its significance. The concept of reinstatement is of outstanding importance. It stems directly from appraising Bowlby's data on the repression of an attachment-need in early infancy. And it implies that the rule of abstinence may no longer be central to psychoanalysis. The concept of corrective emotional experience – the reinstatement and fulfilment of legitimate developmental needs through the medium of a renewed attachment – must take its place as a legitimate, and often major, focus of therapy.

Freud speaks of the transference in terms of pathology: 'this latest creation of the disease which is to be combated like all the earlier ones'.[53] We agree that aspects of pathology may well be transferred onto the person of the analyst. At the same time, we must insist that legitimate developmental needs may likewise be transferred. There is nothing pathological about these needs as such, and thus they are not to be combated, removed, or destroyed, since this can only perpetuate the problem of their lack of fulfilment. Freud alternatively speaks of the transference as creating 'an intermediate region between illness and real life through which the transition from the one to the other is made'.[54] For Freud himself this statement again implies that the transference is an illness, albeit an 'artificial illness'.[55] In terms of our own model, the transference may be regarded as intermediate and transitional insofar as it reinstates the developmental timetable from the point at which its fulfilment was checked. By reinstatement, the transference can make possible the 'transition' from the fixation points of early development to increased developmental fulfilment. In other words, we take transition to imply simply the reparative resumption and fulfilment of the normal developmental process.

Transference neuroses do not 'originate from the ego's refusing to accept a powerful instinctual impulse in the id'.[56] The ego protects the instinctual impulse from the hurtful love-object, but this protection means that – while protected – the instinctual impulse cannot be fulfilled for the time being. When a repressed attachment-need is reinstated, it is improper to state that this transference 'replaces in the patient's mind the desire to be cured'.[57] This is to draw a false antithesis, since cure itself implies the fulfilment of unmet developmental needs. It is true that in the transference 'the whole readiness for these feelings is derived from elsewhere',[58] but this is not to deny the validity of such feelings. The rationale for therapy stems from the recognition that such needs were not previously fulfilled and still require fulfilment. After all, if these needs had been previously fulfilled elsewhere, the therapist would be redundant.

The repetition of 'earlier reactions' and 'infantile prototypes'[59] in the transference is undeniable, but is an incomplete statement of the significance of the transference. The 're-experiencing [of] emotional relations which had their origin in his earliest object-attachments'[60] proves on our data to be a two-sided phenomenon: reproducing early conflict, and reinstating early needs whose fulfilment was checked through conflict. Only in the former case may the transference be regarded as a 'weapon of the resistance'[61] or an 'obstacle'.[62] In the latter, it is nothing of the sort. Likewise, the potential of the transference for becoming the 'best instrument of the analytic treatment'[63] does not refer solely to the interpretation of resistances. Outstandingly, it refers to the transference as a renewed attachment through which developmental needs may now be fulfilled. Interpretation and the overcoming of resistances are important as facilitating this goal, and not otherwise.

Freud stated that the characteristics of the transference are due not to psychoanalysis, but to the neurosis itself[64] – or, as we should prefer to state it, to the patient's psychological condition in both its pathological *and* its developmental aspects. Where developmental needs are involved, the transference can only be dissolved if the needs in question are actually fulfilled. If the transference is interrupted short of such fulfilment, the needs remain unfulfilled or only partially fulfilled. Thus – it must be emphasized – the problem itself continues to a greater or lesser degree unresolved. Likewise, the idea that the transference proves that adults 'have not overcome their former childish dependence' must be interpreted with caution. The persistence of early developmental needs for dependence may well become evident in the transference. However, such needs are not to be *overcome* – any more than an actual child should *overcome* his attachment-needs – but should be *fulfilled*. The developmental problem of unfulfilled needs will persist if it is not met on its own terms.

In this connection, we may reassess Freud's use of the terms 'real' and 'reality', and in particular will suggest that his comments tend to beg the question. In the transference, it is stated, a person 'is flung out of his real relation to the doctor'.[65] However, the persistence of unfulfilled developmental needs is an entirely real fact of contemporary intrapsychic reality. The intrapsychic is as real as the external world; and if early developmental needs have persisted unfulfilled into adult life, they are thereby still a fact of *contemporary* experience. To denote them archaic or anachronistic does not imply that they are illusory or no longer valid, but merely acknowledges that they were not fulfilled at the expected point on the developmental timetable. When such needs are transferred into a contemporary relationship, this implies the reinstatement of a developmentally helpful relationship. As such, it is no more unreal than the actual parent–child relationship is unreal. It is simply a different kind of relationship, where the fulfilment of pre-adult needs takes priority.

Transference love does not, in this sense, involve much disregard for reality.[66] On the contrary, it implies an accurate statement of intrapsychic reality, especially in such aspects as are unresolved or unfulfilled. If a person 'cannot get free of the past', this is not to be equated with a 'neglect [of] what is real and immediate'.[67] The intrapsychic problem is as real and immediate as anything in the external world, and must be treated as such. If, for example, an apparent regression of the libido takes place, this does not imply that the 'attraction of reality has diminished',[68] but only that the intrapsychic reality of incomplete development has become more apparent. This intrapsychic reality may be unfortunate, but it is not thereby unreal.

The external world is not unreal, but it is not the only aspect of reality, and hence it is unfortunate that Freud tends to equate the concepts of reality and of the external world. A contrast between external reality and internal reality would be more accurate. Freud's one-sided use of the term 'reality' is evident in his formulations on neurosis. In a variety of statements, he indicates that the ego is in conflict with the id, under the influence of 'reality',[69] or the 'external world',[70] or the 'real world',[71] or 'external reality'.[72] Here 'reality' and 'the external' are confused. In any case, we have already indicated that the poles of the conflict are *not* the ego and the id. Rather, the ego protects the instinctual impulse from external reality (the love-object perceived as hurtful). In repression, the ego does act 'under the influence of external reality'.[73] But the protective motive is misunderstood when Freud insists that 'the ego is obliged to guard against certain instinctual impulses in the id and to treat them as dangers'.[74] The ego's protective manoeuvre is both realistic and adaptive, but the persistence of this manoeuvre renders it maladaptive, since the needs that it protects still require to be met; and until they are met, through the medium of a restored attachment, developmental fulfilment is impaired.

We may agree that 'the ego, in the service of [external] reality, suppresses a piece of the id',[75] provided that this is understood as protection *of* the id, not protection *from* the id. The behaviour of the ego results in an alteration in the instinctual process,[76] and the ego has thereby 'inhibited and damaged the particular part of the id concerned'.[77] However, Freud also notes that the ego is 'intimately bound up with the id',[78] so that the ego 'can only fend off an instinctual danger by restricting its own organisation'.[79] I wish to suggest that this statement of restriction is both truer and of greater significance than Freud himself realized. Whether the ego is taken to develop out of the id itself[80] or out of an undifferentiated matrix (Hartmann 1939), I would suggest that the growth of the ego as a structure – as distinct from certain autonomous apparatuses – is intimately linked with the vicissitudes of instinctual fulfilment, whereby developmental needs are met or not. To the extent that significant developmental needs are not met, the ego remains undeveloped, even if certain of its cognitive and perceptual capacities develop autonomously and on schedule.

I am not at present convinced that it makes much difference whether one speaks of an original id or an undifferentiated ego-id matrix, since in both cases – the latter as much as the former – the emphasis is placed on the subsequent development of the ego. I am therefore still happy to use Freud's own terminology, and speak of the ego as 'the external, peripheral layer of the id',[81] a 'portion of the id',[82] or 'the better organised part of the id'.[83] The ego 'was developed out of the id by the continual influence of the external world'.[84] The id 'under the influence of the real external world' becomes ego.[85] How is this process achieved? Precisely through the fulfilment of attachment-needs. On this perspective, the two accounts of how the ego is formed prove to be identical:

'According to the first account, the ego is an agency of adaptation which differentiates itself from the id on contact with external reality. Alternatively it is described as the product of identifications culminating in the formation, within the personality, of a love-object cathected by the id.'

(Laplanche and Pontalis 1980: 130)

The decisive 'contact with external reality' lies in the cathexis of external love-objects. And, as I have argued in *Psychogenesis*, the crucial factor for the process of identification lies in the capacity for attachment. I speak of identification-through-attachment, both for the formation of gender identity and for the formation of the ego itself. Thus, contact with external reality, through an attachment, itself implies the forwarding of the identificatory process within the personality. It is not for the id to cathect an internal love-object. Rather, the id cathects external love-objects; and, through receiving love from external love-objects, the ego is formed and built up. The sense of self and of self-worth is received *from others*, and hence too the contrast between narcissism and object-love is rendered redundant.

Freud's understanding of narcissism has of course been much developed in recent years by Heinz Kohut, whose work will be discussed in some detail later on. Here, as a preliminary statement, I wish to comment briefly on Freud's own formulations. One of his favourite images is that of the ego as a 'great reservoir' of libido from which 'object-cathexes are sent out and into which they are withdrawn once more'.[86] I wish to suggest certain reservations about this image and its implications. The young child has a 'great reservoir' of libidinal *needs*, but these needs require *fulfilment*. This fulfilment is obtained through the medium of object-cathexes. In this way, the withdrawal of object-cathexes can only mean a lack of libidinal fulfilment, a lack of actualization. The reservoir image can all too easily have connotations of a 'full storehouse' – though it could equally imply an empty receptacle, which cannot fill itself, but must be filled from outside. Freud's 'amoeba' image[87] seems likewise to do insufficient justice to the inchoate and as-yet-unactualized character of early development and early intrapsychic structure. A 'narcissistic libidinal cathexis of the ego'[88] is not the original state of the child. Precisely because the ego is only in the process of formation, the child does not as yet have an independent psychological existence and is totally dependent on the external world for the fulfilment of its narcissistic needs. Object-cathexes, of however primitive a form, are the channels through which libidinal fulfilment may be received. Attachment to, and dependency on, the object – in its role as auxiliary ego – are the means through which intrapsychic structure is gradually formed. On these grounds, I would criticize such a statement of Freud's as this:

> 'At the very beginning, all the libido is accumulated in the id, while the ego is still in process of formation or is still feeble. The id sends part of this libido out into erotic object-cathexes, whereupon the ego, now grown stronger, tries to get hold of this object-libido and to force itself on the id as a love-object.'[89]

To rephrase this: at the beginning, all libidinal *potential* and libidinal *need* are in the id. The ego is still in process of formation and feeble. The id sends out object-cathexes in order to inaugurate the fulfilment of libidinal needs, whereupon the ego begins to develop precisely through this fulfilment of attachment-needs. The ego does not attempt to divert the id's libido from objects to itself. The ego receives its own fulfilment – indeed, its very formation – through the medium of object-cathexes. The ego cannot very early satisfy the instincts itself. The ego very early exists only in potential, and itself grows only within the matrix of instinctual satisfaction. Love is to be received from the *object*, not from the id. The ego cannot provide what it is itself dependent on for its very formation.

Narcissistic libido is not transformed into object libido.[90] Rather, object-cathexes are the medium for the fulfilment of libidinal needs – of narcissistic needs themselves. Narcissism coincides, not with egoism, [91] but with object-libidinal fulfilment. Pathological narcissism correspondingly stems from lack of object-libidinal fulfilment, where the need for self-esteem becomes clamant precisely because it has not been met.

The concept of identification-through-attachment – developed in *Psychogenesis* – implies that it is misleading to draw a sharp contrast between identification and object-love. Freud states that the two are indistinguishable in the oral phase,[92] but his most frequent statement is to contrast the two.[93] He speaks of identification as the preliminary stage of object-choice,[94] to which object-choice may regress.[95] I would suggest an ongoing complementarity between object-choice and identification: that identification takes place through object-libidinal fulfilment, as does narcissism. Or, in other words, that self-identity and the sense of self are as much mediated through object-libidinal fulfilment as is the sense of self-esteem. Indeed, these are but two facets of the same process. The link will doubtless be of greater intensity in the earlier stages of development, especially the oral stage, but the findings of *Psychogenesis* suggest that the link persists – though in gradually lessening degree – throughout the developmental process towards adulthood.

In addition, I would suggest that it is highly misleading to speak of ego-identifications as the precipitates of *abandoned* object-cathexes.[96] Identification takes place through attachment – through the medium of an *ongoing* object-cathexis. Identifications are the precipitates of *fulfilled* object-cathexes, not *abandoned* ones. The difference in emphasis is crucial. Premature disruption in, or abandonment of, an object-cathexis can only check the identificatory process, not further it. Indeed, as *Psychogenesis* argues, such a check may result in actual *dis*identification: not merely incompletion of identification, but an aversion to further identification – specifically, an aversion to the object and to further attachment to it, such attachment being itself identificatory.

The ego does indeed 'contain the history of [its] object-choices'.[97] However, although object-libidinal needs may be fulfilled, and the relationship *therefore* outgrown, the abandonment of an object-cathexis short of such fulfilment can only be a check to development, and not its furtherance. Where an object-cathexis has been prematurely abandoned, it must be resumed. This is comparable to what we said earlier, that where an attachment-need has been repressed, it is important to facilitate a renewed attachment. Nothing less than this can solve the problem as it actually is.

This in turn suggests the entire legitimacy and validity of what Masterson and Rinsley choose to call a 'chronic overdependence upon external objects' (1975: 164). If the borderline – *a fortiori* the psychotic – presents a massive object-hunger or intense object-dependence, I would suggest – on the basis of the foregoing discussion – that this is an accurate reflection of his intrapsychic state and level of development. An attachment-need was repressed in early years and hence has persisted unfulfilled. Under these circumstances, the intense need for external objects *is still phase-appropriate*. To interpret such needs is merely to acknowledge their presence, and does nothing of itself to meet them – since, by definition, attachment-needs can only be fulfilled through the medium of an actual attachment and not otherwise.

Masterson and Rinsley consider the 'persistence of the wish for reunion' to be a 'defence against . . . abandonment depression' (1975: 170). This would seem to be a notable misinterpretation of the data. The desire for reunion is the reparative attempt to restore attachment (a reunion with the object). Reparation is certainly not defence. On the contrary, a reparative attachment marks the undoing or bypassing of the defensive manoeuvre that originally disrupted attachment and repressed the attachment-need. If the reparative attempt does not take place, or does not succeed, the person in question may experience 'abandonment depression' (an awareness that the needful bond with the object has been missing). But the reparative attempt is cure, not defence. And the 'reality of separation' is itself the problem that requires resolution, precisely through the reinstatement of an object-attachment. Acquiescence in the reality of separation can only imply acquiescence in the persistence of the problem. It is not that the 'pathological ego denies the reality of separation'. It is the acknowledgement of separation (repression of the attachment-need) that itself logically leads to the entirely realistic desire for reunion (the much-needed reinstatement of attachment).

In his discussion of instincts, Freud suggested that 'need' is a better term for an instinctual stimulus,[98] and he stated that 'what does away with a need is satisfaction'.[99] Unfortunately, he speaks of this satisfaction in highly ambivalent terms. Satisfaction 'can only be obtained by removing the state of stimulation at the source of the instinct'.[100] We would prefer to state, unambiguously, that satisfaction depends on the fulfilment of the given need, *which in turn* alters or removes the stimulus impelling towards satisfaction. Freud's own formulations are open to the interpretation that mere tampering with the signals given by stimuli would be adequate, even in the absence of the actual satisfaction of the instinctual need. If such an interpretation seems whimsical or unlikely, I wish to point out that this error occurs whenever attachment-needs are left ungratified. *Only* the actual satisfaction of the given need – through the medium of a renewed attachment – is adequate to the resolution of the problem. The analytic data that we have discussed – above all, Bowlby's paradigm – suggest that gratification – corrective emotional experience and the satisfaction of transference needs – is a valid and important part of the therapeutic endeavour. It should therefore receive due recognition as such.

2

Transference

Freud drew a distinction between the transference neuroses and the narcissistic – or non-transference – neuroses,[1] the latter covering such psychopathology as the functional psychoses. The supposed near-objectlessness of psychotics has been steadily questioned since Freud, and evidence has accumulated that transferences do arise even here. (Fromm-Reichmann 1939; Federn 1953; Sechehaye 1956; Rosenfeld 1969; Arlow 1971). Absence of transference was classically linked with non-analysability. While therapeutic pessimism persists (Kernberg 1969; Kohut 1971; Arieti 1974), many have been prepared to use modified techniques for more serious cases of pathology (Federn 1953; Zetzel 1956; Balint 1960; Little 1966; Blanck and Blanck 1974; Lidz 1975). Indeed, it has been stated that classical analytic technique should be reserved for the neuroses alone (Blanck and Blanck 1974). The potential for transference and the potential for analysability are important sets of data, and I would argue that they have been insufficiently correlated with each other. In the functional psychoses and borderline states, it is the nature of the transference that must – logically – suggest the nature of the technique used, and not vice versa. If the classical directives for technique do not do justice to new data, the technique must be modified – not the significance of the data ignored or reduced until it fits the original model.

The meaning of 'transference neuroses' has changed since Freud's original formulation. Since transferences appear within a wide range of psychopathology, many disorders could be referred to as 'transference neuroses' (disorders in which transferences may appear). But not all transference disorders are *neuroses* in the contemporary use of the word. For Freud, the neuroses and the transference disorders coincided, and he used one term for both. We must bear in mind that the latter category has been vastly extended, and must make clear which sense we mean – or do not mean – when we echo Freud's language. For Freud, the contrast lay between the transference disorders and the psychoses. We may contrast the neuroses and the psychoses, but see transferences in both. Both are transference disorders ('transference neuroses' in Freud's original sense). Thus, too, we may speak of transference psychoses, which for Freud would have been a mere contradiction in terms.

In addition, 'transference neurosis' has generally been interpreted to mean transference *as* neurosis, transference *as* pathology (whether neurotic or some more serious disorder). Here I wish to add my own comment that, although transference is to be found *in* many mental disorders, it is not necessarily to be equated with pathology in itself. Transference may well involve the replication of early conflict, but – equally – we have seen that it may mark the reinstatement of a repressed attachment-need, i.e. a legitimate developmental need, not pathology.

Where an attachment-need is involved, we have stated that interpretation is insufficient: only a restored attachment can deal with the problem on its own terms. Unfortunately, since Eissler's paper on technique, originally presented in 1953, any

modification of technique has been regarded as a 'parameter' –
'the deviation, both quantitative and qualitative, from the basic
model technique, that is to say, from a technique which requires interpretation as the exclusive tool' (1980: 382). The
importance and centrality of interpretation is emphasized as
'the baseline of psychoanalytic technique' (1980: 399). And this
emphasis is reinforced by Eissler's insistence that 'a parameter
is to be used only when it finally leads to its self-elimination;
that is to say, the final phase of the treatment must always
proceed with a parameter of zero' (1980: 383). However, we
have already indicated that interpretation does not and cannot
of itself fulfil an unmet developmental need for attachment. The
classical model for technique does not fit the further analytic
data provided by Bowlby's paradigm, and it must therefore be
regarded as a limited model, not the sole norm for analytic
technique. It is therefore highly unsatisfactory to speak of
different techniques as 'parameters' and 'deviations' when – by
the very nature of the psychopathology – they must constitute
the main part of the therapy and are directly relevant to the
most central focus of concern.

Freud's therapeutic goal of making the unconscious
conscious[2] is a valid goal but may not be the sole focus of the
therapeutic endeavour. It is, by definition, important where
lack of conscious awareness constitutes a major part of the
problem. Where the essential problem is different, the therapeutic goal must likewise be modified. In addition, it is important to note that 'making the unconscious conscious' is not in
fact equivalent to Freud's dictum 'where id was, there ego shall
be'.[3] The two are often treated as identical, but this is to
misunderstand the way in which the ego is formed. Making the
unconscious conscious may enhance the cognitive functioning
of the ego, but it does not of itself contribute to the structuralization of the ego. The formation of the ego as such – as distinct
from certain autonomous ego-functions – takes place as id-
needs are fulfilled through object-cathexes. Object-libidinal
fulfilment is the medium of intrapsychic structuralization.
Object-cathexes providing the fulfilment of attachment-needs

are thus essential to the goal 'where id was, there ego shall be'.

With Fairbairn (1952) I see libido as intrinsically object-seeking. With Bowlby (1969, 1973), I insist on the importance of attachment-needs, and consider the consequences of their repression. When an attachment-need has been repressed, we must seek to restore an id-object link, not an id-ego link. The id-object link is essential, though this in turn leads to the further structuralization of the ego. (Thus, one may speak of an indirect id-ego link, via the object; a triadic, not a dyadic, link.)

In this connection, it is interesting to note Kohut's comments on the transference as originally bearing an intrapsychic rather than interpersonal connotation. He says that 'transference in the narrower sense . . . is not an interpersonal phenomenon but is basically the expression of an intrapsychic conflict',[4] viz. a conflict between the ego and the id, not the ego and the outer world. In our discussion of repression we have already indicated that the ego represses the id-impulse in order to protect it from an unsatisfactory object (the outer world). The conflict is interpersonal – its consequences are endopsychic. But the latter has no meaning apart from the former, and so one cannot logically speak of a 'narrower sense' of transference. Transference does involve 'the influence of the primary process on the secondary process'[5], as Freud himself noted,[6] but this is not the total phenomenon of transference, only a certain aspect of it. Here, as previously, one must insist on the importance of the id-object link, rather than the id-ego link. However, the full interpersonal dimension of the transference still has not been realized. In practice, the phenomenon is treated as merely endopsychic when attachment-needs are not fulfilled. Interpretation and the attainment of insight do not by themselves do justice to the interpersonal dimension of intrapsychic needs.

It is of value to make clear the dynamic meaning of significant displacements from the past in the present – but it is vital to follow through by taking such meaning seriously. An unfulfilled attachment-need must be fulfilled, not merely interpreted (since when has diagnosis by itself been tantamount to cure?) There is no reason why such a transference should be 'dissolved' by interpretation (Fenichel 1941; Kohut 1978). A correct interpretation may well make true connections, but this will merely illustrate the nature of the need. A need does not disappear merely by pointing out the fact of its existence. The relation between past and present is of crucial importance here. The rationale for eliminating the transference by interpretation has been stated thus: 'When the ego recognizes and sorts out the confusion between past and present, transference dissolves' (Blanck and Blanck 1974: 136). The logic of this statement is fair, but its basic datum is incorrect. The transference does not only or necessarily involve a *confusion* between past and present. If early needs have persisted unmet into adult years, they remain genuinely contemporary needs – current needs, even if archaic in nature. The reinstatement of early needs does not imply any kind of confusion – it merely marks the resumption of the developmental timetable, from the point at which it was left off. To resume the fulfilment of developmental needs is not a 'misunderstanding of the present in terms of the past' (Fenichel 1941: 67). It is based on the clear understanding that these needs were not met in the past, and that they may be met in the present. A transfer from past to present – or reinstatement of the past in the present – does not necessarily imply distortions in the perceptions of reality (Langs 1978). It *is* a displacement, but it is not on that account 'relatively inappropriate' (Langs 1978: 151). A greater or lesser degree of distortion may at times be present, but this is not a necessary feature of the transference. To reinstate the fulfilment of unmet developmental needs is highly therapeutic. It is belated, rather than distorted, though distortion may be involved in the reanimation of early conflicts.

It is true that the patient can 'work through unrealistic transference relations with the analyst' (Guntrip 1961: 415). In addition, we would insist that he can work through and fulfil realistic transference relations with the analyst, viz. to fulfil legitimate developmental needs through the medium of a renewed attachment. The contrast drawn between responses as 'appropriate (realistic) or inappropriate (based more upon the past and therefore, transference)' (Langs 1978: 165) marks a false dichotomy. Transference responses may be entirely appropriate and realistic if they involve the remobilization of unfulfilled developmental needs. It is not merely repressed fantasy (Curtis 1980; Langs 1978) that may be projected onto objects in current reality, but actual attachment-needs. In such an instance, interpretation may not be equated with handling the transference by rational means (Kepecs 1966), but is a highly irrational manoeuvre. Only a restored attachment can meet an attachment-need; interpretation can at most increase awareness of the (unmet) need.

Langs (1978) regards gratifications of the transference as irrational, in that they undermine conflict resolution. Such a statement misunderstands the two kinds of therapeutic goal at issue. Conflict resolution *is* important, but it does not stand alone. The repression of an attachment-need prevents the fulfilment of that need. But the undoing of repression is merely a first step to the larger goal of restoring attachment. If the attachment-need is not actually met, then the therapist's un-willingness to meet the need becomes as much an obstacle to fulfilment as repression itself once was. An interpersonal barrier takes the place of an intrapsychic barrier, and may be equally effective. The analytic 'rule of abstinence' is not merely meaningless, but directly counter-therapeutic, where a repressed and unfulfilled attachment-need is the problem at issue.

It may be noted in this connection that Kohut's admirable work on the restoration of the self is marred by his endorsement of the rule of abstinence. He speaks of the need to make childhood wishes conscious, but to keep them frustrated and unsatisfied.[7] The possibility of evasion by renewed repression is blocked, and therefore there is only one way left: 'increasing integration into the mature and reality-adapted sectors and segments of the psyche'[8] as 'the psyche is forced to create new structures'.[9] On the basis of our preceding discussion, this seems illogical. The only way left is for the unmet need to persist unmet, albeit in a state of increased awareness. New structures only develop through the fulfilment of object-libidinal needs. If such fulfilment is blocked, structuralization cannot take place – or may happen to do so in practice only if the analysand gets more out of the relationship than the analyst intends to give! Kohut speaks of the analytic process as keeping 'the infantile need activated while simultaneously cutting off all roads except the one towards maturation and realistic employment'.[10] Unfortunately, by his own account, he has deliberately cut off the essential road to maturation, if he is unwilling to provide gratification for unfulfilled attachment-needs. Repression was significant *only* as a hindrance to the fulfilment of attachment-needs. The undoing of repression is significant *only* as a preliminary to the fulfilment of attachment-needs.

Kohut distinguishes structural transferences from narcissistic or selfobject transferences. Transference proper (as he regards the structural transference) involves three characteristics: a repressed infantile drive, repetition, and confusion of the old and the new object.[11] All three characteristics are to be found in the neuroses, but narcissistic personality disorders manifest only the two latter.[12] I have already indicated some criticism of how these latter concepts (repetition, confusion) are to be understood. Here I wish to add that the remaining characteristic is most certainly to be found in narcissistic disorders as well. Indeed, it is the most central feature of the whole area of borderline and psychotic disorders, as argued in detail in *Psychogenesis* (Moberly 1983). The drive for attachment is repressed in order to shield it from the object that is experienced as hurtful. The normal need for attachment therefore remains unfulfilled, *and thereby the structuralization of the ego is checked*, since this structuralization is dependent on the object-libidinal fulfilment of id-needs.

In this way, we may modify the contrast drawn by Kohut between the features of neurotic and narcissistic disorders. His amplification of the classical model is most valuable. However, the way in which he presents his data tends to unnecessary dichotomies, where I would wish to argue the case for a closer integration of his concepts.

Narcissistic disorders *do* presuppose a repressed drive seeking fulfilment. This is not to reduce narcissism to the status of a neurosis. The two are qualitatively different, but the nature of the contrast must be carefully expressed. In both instances, not just the one, a repressed drive is seeking satisfaction (or, better, fulfilment). But in the borderline spectrum of pathology, it is entirely correct to link this with a 'narcissistic ego seeking reassurance'.[13] Kohut's affirmation is to be linked with, not separated from, the concept of drive-satisfaction. Id-needs are involved in both instances – indeed, in narcissistic pathology more fundamentally so – since it is through the object-libidinal fulfilment of id-needs that the ego is built up. Conversely ego-weakness or a narcissistic mode of ego-functioning imply a block in id-fulfilment. Kohut states that classical theory is limited by its focus on structural conflict and structural neuroses.[14] I would state that classical theory and Kohut's work alike are limited by an inadequate understanding of the relation between drive-fulfilment and the structuralization of the ego. The two are to be linked, not contrasted.

We may agree with Kohut's distinction between intact structures (in the neuroses) and defective structures (in the narcissistic disorders).[15] However, drive aims and unresolved conflict are involved as much and more in the latter as in the former. It is the repression of the attachment-need that blocks the structuralization of the ego. On this account, it is misleading to contrast 'fear of the drive' with 'the breakup of the self'.[16] Disintegration anxiety stems directly from the fact that the id-need was repressed and therefore remained unfulfilled. The 'needs of a defective self'[17] *are* drive-wishes. Likewise, we may not contrast conflict solution with the establishment of self-cohesion.[18] Repression is to be resolved *in order to* restore attachment and *thereby* to resume the process of the structuralization of the ego, with all that this implies for the sense of self-esteem and personal identity. With Kohut, we may ask how psychoanalysis has been able to use a drive-defence model without a psychology of the self.[19] But there is no need to contrast a mental-apparatus psychology with a self-psychology.[20] The psychology of the self merely expands the implications of the drive-defence-structural model, and we must insist that it remains intimately linked with it.

Drives are not mere 'disintegration products',[21] and conflicts regarding drive aims are not 'secondary in narcissistic personality disorders'.[22] The repressed and unfulfilled drive for attachment is of primary significance, precisely for its effect on the normal process of intrapsychic structuralization. It is outstandingly the narcissistic disorders that involve 'unconscious object-directed strivings, and . . . defenses against them'[23] (or rather, defences *of* them, by protective repression). Kohut's statement is not in fact specific for the neuroses. In addition, we would qualify what he says here by a reminder that interpretation alone is irrelevant to the satisfaction of object-directed strivings, and it does not by itself lead to the expansion of the realm of the ego,[24] except cognitively. Only object-libidinal fulfilment can satisfy such strivings and thereby further structuralize the incomplete and defective ego.

Incidentally, it may be noted that *Psychogenesis* and my use of Bowlby's paradigm suggest that repression is – as Freud originally suggested[25] – an early defence. It is common to speak of it as a later and more sophisticated defence (Fenichel 1945; Kernberg 1976). The present discussion suggests that it is a primary form of defence, and is crucially significant for narcissistic, borderline, and psychotic pathology. Repression does not have to presuppose the differentiation of the mental apparatus into ego and id. The data of *Psychogenesis* clearly imply that the repressive function exists very early, prior to the structuralization of the ego as a whole. And the repression of an attachment-need – retaining it as an unfulfilled id-content – thereby prevents further structuralization of the ego, until such time as the id-object link is resumed.

We may also conclude that the kind of contrast drawn between the respective approaches of Heinz Kohut and Otto Kernberg is again something of a false dichotomy. *Pace* Kohut, narcissistic defects do presuppose conflict and lack of drive fulfilment. *Pace* Kernberg, the defence of what is being warded off is significant for the resultant developmental defects in ego-structuralization. *Pace* both Kohut and Kernberg, the therapeutic goal must – by the very nature of the problem – involve actual object-libidinal fulfilment.

Narcissistic disorders involve conflict as much and more than the neuroses. Narcissistic disorders also involve transference as much and more than the neuroses. Freud's original distinction between the transference-neuroses and the narcissistic, non-transference neuroses has been rehabilitated in the current distinction between transference on the one hand and pre-transference phenomena (variously designated) on the other hand (Kohut 1971; Blanck and Blanck 1979; Stolorow and Lachmann 1980). The capacity for transference is seen as a developmental achievement (Blanck and Blanck 1974, 1979; Stolorow and Lachmann 1980), dependent on the attainment of self and object constancy. When the object-representation is undifferentiated from the self-representation, there is less capacity for transference (Blanck and Blanck 1974). It is the separation of self and object images that makes transference possible (Blanck and Blanck 1979). Stolorow and Lachmann (1980) propose a distinction between the precursors or prestages of transference and its classical form. I would suggest that the classical form may be contrasted with more archaic forms without in any sense regarding the latter as less truly transferences. They are not the precursors of transference, merely earlier forms of (genuine) transference. It is true that 'before . . . separation-individuation . . . there can be only merged self and object representations' (Blanck and Blanck 1977: 39). However, this fact does not justify the conclusion that the capacity for transference is absent. It merely determines the nature of the transference, which in its earlier forms is *necessarily* a selfobject transference, in contrast to the later forms of whole-object transference. But both are equally transference.

Transference occurs when 'preconscious attitudes toward the analyst become the carriers of repressed, infantile, object-directed wishes'.[26] This kind of definition of transference is entirely adequate to cover our concept of the reinstatement of early developmental needs. Transference implies 'what is transferred', and no aspect of what is transferred from an earlier to a later relationship may logically be excluded from the concept of transference. Kohut suggests that 'all transferences are repetitions, not all repetitions are transferences'.[27] He bases this conclusion on the hypothesized absence of a repressed drive in narcissism. I have already proposed that a repressed drive is in fact a central feature of such disorders. There is also a more general criticism of the restriction of the term 'transference'. Transferences are, as Kohut himself suggests, 'defined by preanalytically established internal factors in the analysand's personality structure'.[28] The character of these internal factors will indeed determine the nature of the transference, for the transference makes manifest the level of developmental progress – the level of intrapsychic structuralization and the correlative capacity and need for objects. But at every level and in every instance we see 'what is transferred', i.e. transference. The analyst may function as a 'screen for the projection of internal structure'[29] *to whatever degree internal structure is or is not present.* Internal structure may be relatively mature and intact, or it may be defective or missing in greater or lesser degree. The projection of a *lack* of internal structure is as transferential as is the projection of an intact structure. And, where intrapsychic structure is incomplete, the transference must of necessity be a selfobject transference, where the analyst 'is substituting for . . . psychic structure'.[30] Where there are 'structural defects in the self', 'selfobject transferences . . . establish themselves on the basis of these defects'.[31]

In narcissistic disorders the analyst functions as 'an archaic prestructural object'.[32] He is needed in order to replace the functions of a segment of the mental apparatus which had not been established in childhood.[33] The patient is 'yearning to find a substitute for the missing (or insufficiently developed) psychic structure . . . seeking with addictionlike intensity . . . to establish a relationship to people who serve as stand-ins for the omnipotent idealised selfobject, i.e. to the archaic precursor of the missing inner structure'.[34] This is not the transference of the neurotic but it is the transference stemming from, and making manifest, an earlier developmental level. Or, in Kohut's words, it is 'the direct continuation of an early reality . . . [not] transformed into solid psychological structures'.[35] The function assigned to the analyst is of necessity exactly correlative with the degree of intrapsychic structuralization and object-need in the analysand.

Kohut describes the addictionlike intensity or hunger of the narcissistic personality as 'not due to a craving activated by the drives involved, but by the intense need to fill a structural defect'.[36] This is a false antithesis. This hunger *is* the craving of drives – drives seeking object-libidinal fulfilment, through which intrapsychic structuralization takes place. It is the satisfaction of these drives that will meet the need to fill a structural defect. The analyst is 'experienced within the framework of an archaic interpersonal relationship',[37] and it is precisely as such that he serves as a substitute for psychological structure,[38] since this *is* the function of the object at early stages of development. When the normal developmental timetable has been interrupted, this phase-appropriate need for a selfobject persists into adult years. Thus, to speak of a 'chronic over-dependence upon external objects' (Masterson and Rinsley 1975: 164) in the adult is an unsuitably emotive statement, with pejorative connotations. There *is* a great need for external objects, but this is an accurate reflection of the lack of developmental fulfilment. When a need has persisted unmet into adult years, this *only* implies an interruption in the developmental timetable. It does not – as often assumed – imply that the need as such is inappropriate. On the contrary, the need is still – as it ever was – normal and valid and phase-appropriate (the latter term must refer primarily to the actual state of developmental fulfilment, whether or not such fulfilment may be correlated with chronology).

We may, with Kohut, distinguish selfobjects and whole objects, but would not insist that only the latter are true objects.[39] The term 'whole object' says all that needs to be said, without the emotive overtones of 'true object'. The selfobject may not be an independent, separate object, but he or she is a true object for a particular level of developmental progress. Indeed, no other object than a selfobject *can* be true to, fit with, take up the needs of, the earlier stages of development prior to the attainment of intrapsychic structuralization. However, where the analyst is a selfobject for his patient, it is not right to label this as an 'impersonal function'.[40] It is the personal function appropriate to early developmental needs. The analyst as selfobject has as personal a function as any parent of a small child has a personal function *qua* parent.

Similarly, it marks an unfortunate choice of language that the transference has often been contrasted with a 'real relationship' (Langs 1978: 146; Blanck and Blanck 1979: 99, 101). The reinstatement of early unmet needs in the transference is – on our argument – entirely realistic. Langs states that the analyst should gratify 'realistic needs', not 'primitive needs' (1976: 252). Where intrapsychic structuralization is incomplete, these primitive needs *are* realistic, and it can only be highly unrealistic to ignore such needs or to insist that they do not require fulfilment. (Is the problem incomplete structuralization or is it not?) Likewise, it is inadequate to state that 'the therapist resembles the primary partner from the patient's misperceptions only, because of need for object replication' (Blanck and Blanck 1979: 135). If there is truly a need for object replication, then it is not a question of misperception. There is genuinely a need for a primary partner, and it is realistic to meet this need, if such is the nature of the problem.

Blanck and Blanck ask: 'When is the analyst real, when is he truly a transference figure, when is he experienced as . . . part of a selfobject unit fantasied to be a potential gratifier of unfulfilled need?' (1979: 101). Our answer is that the analyst may be all three at the same time. The contrasts drawn by the Blancks are somewhat misleading. We may rightly contrast transference-relationships with non-transference relationships, but must note the areas of reality in the former as well as in the latter. We may rightly contrast archaic transferences with more mature transferences, but must insist that in each instance the phenomenon is truly a matter of transference, even if indicative of a different level of development.

It is neither adequate nor accurate to speak of 'transference-like structures',[41] or to write off the search for replication of early experience with a primary object as 'pretransference' (Blanck and Blanck 1979: 25). An archaic transference is involved here. We may agree that it is qualitatively different from the kind of transference to be found in the neuroses. At the same time, we would insist that there is no reason to make the phenomena associated with the neuroses normative for the whole range of psychopathology. Transference is not to be defined by such characteristics as are specific for the neuroses alone.

It is not 'transference-like phenomena', but actual transferences, that 'refer to subphase levels of undifferentiation of self from object images' (Blanck and Blanck 1979: 101). The Blancks (1979) call for a term other than transference to describe the introduction of early unmet needs into present relationships. I would instead call for a recognition of the nature of archaic transferences, in which early developmental needs are reinstated. 'Need replication' and 'object replication' (Blanck and Blanck 1979: 106) are vital and legitimate aspects of archaic transferences. If the therapist is treated as 'a potential gratifier of. . . the needs of early subphases of ego organization' (1979: 101), this role stems from the patient's lack of intrapsychic structuralization and his correlative need for structuralizing object-relationships. In such circumstances, an archaic tie *is* needed to substitute for structure, and to provide structure-forming experiences through the medium of a renewed attachment.

The concept of the object as a substitute for structure is crucial to the whole spectrum of more serious psychopathology. The therapist *is* required to function as part of a selfobject unit to gratify need (Blanck and Blanck 1979). This role is necessary – and entirely realistic – precisely because of the nature of the problem, which is one of arrested and incomplete intrapsychic structuralization.

Transference is not to be defined with reference to insight and the capacity for interpretation (Fenichel 1945; Blanck and Blanck 1979). To do this is again to make the neuroses normative. One may, in any case, interpret more archaic transferences and facilitate insight if one so wishes. But this does nothing of itself to dissolve the transferences in question, it merely increases awareness of the needs involved. Two points are of importance. One is that we should recognize the continuity of the phenomenon of transference across a wide spectrum of disorders. The other is that we should respect qualitative differences in the type of transferences and modify our technique accordingly. At present, neither point is accepted. (Neurotic) transference is separated from pre-transference phenomena (archaic transferences). And the technique used for transference in neurosis is in essence made normative for more serious disorders as well.

Kohut states that the goal of psychoanalysis is not just knowledge, making the unconscious conscious; but 'filling in structural defects . . . the restoration of the self'.[42] This is an admirable statement, with which I would entirely agree. Unfortunately, Kohut effectively disqualifies his own statement by his insistence on maintaining the rule of abstinence and ruling out the gratification of narcissistic needs. Indulgence is regarded as 'a temporary tactical requirement'.[43] There may be 'transitorily . . . reluctant compliance with the childhood wish',[44] but the 'true analytic aim is not indulgence but mastery based on insight, achieved in a setting of tolerable analytic abstinence'.[45] However, the fulfilment of unmet developmental needs is not to be reduced to mere compliance with childhood wishes. And there is no reason why such compliance should be transitory or reluctant, if indeed such unmet needs are the very essence of the problem. Kohut in practice retains the very principle that he claims to have superseded, if the analyst is still to interpret and not to gratify.

We may agree with Kohut that structuralization is the

central point at issue. Where we disagree is as regards the process by which structuralization is achieved. Kohut links structuralization – or 'transmuting internalisation'[46] – with 'optimal frustration'.[47] It is losses that lead to the acquisition of new psychic structures, and it is through separation that internal structure is gained (Goldberg 1978). I wish very strongly to dispute this suggestion that internalization is enhanced by object loss.[48] The argument of *Psychogenesis* is that internalization takes place through the medium of an ongoing attachment; that object loss checks the process of internalization; and that internalization may be resumed only through the medium of a restored attachment. Mourning does *not* promote internalization. It may internalize the final phase of the preceding object-relationship, but thereafter no ongoing internalization can take place, because there is no ongoing attachment to the object. It is the *fulfilment* of object-libidinal needs that leads to the structuralization of the ego, not their abrogation.

There is a certain ambiguity in the affirmation that 'psychological structures . . . are built up in consequence of the gradual decathexis of the narcissistically experienced archaic object'.[49] Decathexis does not *lead* to structure formation,[50] but is the *consequence* of structure formation. Conversely, the withdrawal of cathexes prior to the completion of structuralization checks the latter process, at whatever stage has been reached at the time of decathexis. These statements are of crucial importance, since they imply that psychoanalysis in general and Kohut in particular have confused what checks internalization for what promotes it! The object *is* to be relinquished,[51] but *only* when the ongoing need for attachment has been fulfilled. Relinquishment of the object *prior* to such fulfilment checks structuralization. It is the fulfilment of object-libidinal needs – not deprivation[52] that turns the object into an introject. We agree with Kohut that the goal is 'the acquisition of permanent psychological structures, which continue endopsychically the functions that had previously been fulfilled by the idealized object'.[53] But we most emphatically disagree that 'structure formation is always due to a loss of the prestructural selfobject'.[54] Loss can only check structuralization. It is an ongoing attachment to the prestructural selfobject – a continuing cathexis, not a decathexis – that promotes internalization.

Kohut regards a narcissistic defect as the 'result of a chronic lack of structure-forming experiences of optimal frustration during the pre-oedipal period'.[55] We would ascribe such a defect precisely to frustration, loss, decathexis, the repression of an attachment-need. Kohut states that 'if the optimal transmuting internalisation of the idealised selfobject is interfered with, then the idealised object is retained as an archaic prestructural object'.[56] Less ambiguously, it is not the archaic object that is retained, but the *need* for such an object – a need that still requires to be fulfilled if internalization is to be resumed, maintained, and completed. Incomplete structure is exactly correlative with the persisting need for the cathexis of a selfobject. Merely to acknowledge such a need, while frustrating its direct satisfaction, does not leave open the path to maturity,[57] but very effectively blocks it. 'Further psychic development through structure building'[58] can only take place through object-libidinal fulfilment. If unmet developmental needs are at issue, they must be met (fulfilled, gratified), not merely acknowledged or interpreted. Or, as we stated previously, when an attachment-need is repressed, the problem lies in the attachment-need remaining unfulfilled. The undoing of repression is not a goal in itself, but merely a step towards the overall goal of resuming the actual fulfilment of attachment-needs.

An ongoing attachment to the selfobject is the medium of intrapsychic structuralization. It is not only the conclusions of *Psychogenesis*, but Kohut's own data, that support this proposition. The very function of the selfobject, as described by Kohut, implies this. Selfobjects function 'in the service of the self' or as 'part of the self'.[59] They serve as a 'substitute' for missing psychological structure.[60] It is because structuralization was checked that there persists an 'intense need to fill a structural defect', marked by an 'addictionlike intensity of . . . hunger'[61] for a selfobject. A 'milieu of empathic selfobjects *is* . . . [the]

self'.[62] The selfobject *is* 'the child's psychological structure'[63] and the preceding references from Kohut suggest that the selfobject is equally the psychological structure of the developmentally affronted adult. Kohut's own data – if taken seriously, as they stand – suggest the importance of the need for the selfobject. When an attachment to the selfobject is reinstated, the incomplete self begins to receive the support it needs. 'Union with the . . . selfobject' leads to 'narcissistic peace' and 'a clinical picture of improved functioning'.[64] Likewise, 'narcissistic equilibrium depends on the analysand's narcissistic relationship to an archaic, narcissistically experienced, prestructural selfobject'.[65] Conversely, the unavailability of a selfobject tie has adverse consequences for the incompletely structuralized self. Loss or absence of the selfobject results in – or, better, makes apparent – the fragmentation of the self.[66] Such loss is a 'threat to [the] experience of the continuity of [the] self',[67] since the selfobject substitutes for the structure that has not yet been attained. It was decathexis of the selfobject (repression of the attachment-need) that originally checked the process of structuralization, and caused the need for the selfobject to persist unmet into adult years. If, when a selfobject transference arises, the therapeutic goal is seen as decathexis of the selfobject, this can only result in the reinstatement of the original problem! A renewed attachment to a selfobject marks the *inauguration* of the solution, the *beginning* of the resumption of the developmental process – but this process must be carried through and not checked yet again. It is not infantile fantasy, but a genuine and unmet developmental need, that is at issue. Decathexis prior to the fulfilment of attachment-needs must therefore be regarded as illogical and countertherapeutic, in view of the nature of the problem. It is the *fulfilment* of attachment-needs that will in due course *result* in the decathexis of the selfobject. 'Transmuting internalisation' takes place *through the medium of* a selfobject transference.

3

Selfobjects
and
structuralization

Kohut presents a detailed discussion of narcissistic transferences or – as he later denotes them – selfobject transferences.
The 'idealized parent imago' may be remobilized in an 'idealizing transference'. And the 'grandiose self' may be remobilized
in a 'mirror transference'.[1] Both are forms of selfobject transference, which may be further classified into three types according
to developmental considerations.[2] In all three, the analyst is 'a
figure . . . of object-constancy in the narcissistic realm . . .
however primitive the object may be; and with the aid of this
more or less stable narcissistically invested object, the transference contributes . . . to the maintenance of the cohesiveness of
the self'.[3] I wish to emphasize here that Kohut's statement is to
be taken quite literally. It *is* the transference that helps to
maintain the cohesiveness of the self. Or – in other words – it *is*
the renewed attachment to the selfobject that further promotes
the structuralization of the incomplete ego, through the belated
fulfilment of essential object-libidinal needs.

I would take seriously the search for replicating early experience as the valid and vital attempt to reinstate the fulfilment of early needs. These needs were not fulfilled according to the normal developmental timetable, and hence have persisted unmet and still require to be met. Kohut speaks of narcissistic transferences as the activation of a developmental stage.[4] They are based on

> 'therapeutic regression to precisely that point where the normal development of the psychic structures of the self was interrupted. . . . The analytic situation . . . brings about a reactivation of that developmental point in time at which the basic disorder began. Thus, the interrupted psychological growth process is given the opportunity to continue beyond the point of its arrest'.[5]

The narcissistic or selfobject transference is therefore itself the 'driving force toward developmental progress of the damaged self'.[6] I accept these affirmations of Kohut as they stand, without the further qualifications he himself provides, which to my mind effectively disqualify these statements. The two main points made here are: (a) The selfobject transference marks the reactivation of an early developmental stage. I would add that this reactivation does not imply intensification or distortion. (b) This transference will promote further growth and structuralization. I would add that this requires the recognition that the renewed attachment to the selfobject is itself the medium for further structuralization. The transference is to be maintained, in order that object-libidinal needs may be fulfilled.

As regards the first point, Kohut speaks of 'the (albeit distorted) activation in reverse of certain archaic normal stages of earliest mental development'.[7] He states that in the transference there is not a normal but an intensified and distorted wish or need.[8] These suggestions of intensification and distortion do not seem to be justified on the evidence that Kohut himself presents. What his evidence undoubtedly presents is the *intensity* of the given need. But intensity does not necessarily imply *intensification*, i.e. an *increase* in intensity. What I wish to suggest is that this intensity of need is normal for early or arrested stages of development. Where intrapsychic structuralization is still only inchoate, an attachment to a selfobject – an external substitute for structure – is essential for psychological survival. A 'milieu of empathic selfobjects *is* [the] self'.[9] Intensity of need for a selfobject is therefore the accurate and normal correlate of incomplete self-structuralization. There is no evidence for regressive alteration here.[10] Nor does the admixture of aggressive elements[11] in the transference imply distortion. It may be adequately explained by recalling that the attachment-need – normal in itself – was repressed by a defensive manoeuvre *vis-à-vis* the hurtful object. However, the hostility or admixture of aggressiveness involved in defence in no way impugns the legitimacy of the attachment-need. The two points are separate issues – a defensive manoeuvre, and the need that is defended.

Kohut speaks of an intensified and distorted need, which cannot be tolerated and is therefore repressed or disavowed and split off.[12] By contrast, I would speak of the repression of a normal attachment-need, which results in this – the child's naturally intense need for a selfobject – remaining unmet. Structuralization thereby remains incomplete, and cannot continue until a structuralizing attachment to a selfobject has been reinstated.

Intensity of early developmental needs is normal. I would likewise wish to reinterpret Kohut's use of the terms 'grandiose' and 'idealising'. It is not a 'grandiose self' but a very needy (and incomplete) self that is at issue. It is not grandiosity, but a realistic awareness of developmental incompletion, that results in an insatiable hunger[13] for the love of a selfobject. Kohut states that the therapist must confront 'grandiose fantasies with a realistic conception of the self' leading to the realization that life offers only limited possibilities for the gratification of narcissism.[14] It is entirely realistic to be aware of the great needs of the incomplete self (needs for a structuralizing object-libidinal attachment). Life may offer only limited gratification of adult pride and ambition, but we are speaking here of legitimate pre-adult developmental needs, which are –

normally – gratified during the course of the developmental process. Again, Kohut states that the 'unresponded-to self has not been able to transform its archaic grandiosity and its archaic wish to merge with an omnipotent selfobject into reliable self-esteem'.[15] It is not the wish for merger, but the *need* for a selfobject, that is at issue; and such a need can only be met through an actual attachment to a selfobject. In the absence of this, the *inchoate* self must perforce remain incomplete and needy. Moreover, the goal is not the building of self-esteem, but the actual structuralization of the ego. Self-esteem is merely a consequence of this structuralization and not an independent goal.

The 'idealising' of the selfobject seems likewise to be no more than a realistic awareness of the great need for the selfobject at the given developmental stage. Kohut speaks of the need to withdraw idealizing cathexes (see in a more realistic light) and employ them in the formation of psychic structure.[16] However, it was the withdrawal of cathexes (repression of the attachment-need) that resulted in the persistence of the great need for a selfobject. It is not the 'lack of opportunity to discover . . . realistic shortcomings',[17] but the absence of attachment, that results in 'continuing idealisation'[18] – the continuing need for an idealized selfobject. And recathexis, not decathexis,[19] is the means for further structure formation. The idealized parent imago is 'unaltered'[20] because the need it represents – for an ongoing selfobject attachment – has not yet been fulfilled. This need is not a fantasy to be modified,[21] but a developmental need to be fulfilled. Continued yearning[22] implies that the need has not yet been met, and still requires to be met.

Incomplete structuralization implies that archaic needs persist into adult life. Kohut speaks of fixation 'on archaic grandiose self configurations and/or on archaic, overestimated, narcissistically cathected objects',[23] and further states that these hinder adult activities by the 'intrusion of the archaic structures'.[24] But these archaic structures *are* the self in the developmentally affronted adult – the self which is incomplete and therefore still requires selfobjects. Adult activities are hindered by the fact of developmental incompletion, by the fact that the person is not yet – in this respect – adult. The therapeutic goal is not to integrate repressed narcissistic structures 'into the realistic segments of the total personality'.[25] The narcissistic structures are in any case entirely realistic to the limited stage of development that has actually been reached (it is not objective to equate 'realistic' with 'mature'). The therapeutic goal must be to undo repression and fulfil narcissistic object-libidinal needs, thereby promoting further structuralization.

The central anxiety in narcissism is seen as the 'fear of the dedifferentiating intrusion of the narcissistic structures and their energies into the ego'.[26] This statement of Kohut's tends to beg the question. In narcissism, the ego – apart from its autonomous functions – *essentially consists of these narcissistic structures*, precisely because structuralization is incomplete. Dedifferentiation is a correlate of incomplete structuralization, in that the inchoate ego still to a greater or lesser degree requires a selfobject. It is hardly surprising that the 'grandiose self' is 'retained in its unaltered form and strives for the fulfilment of its archaic aims'.[27] These archaic aims are phase-appropriate for the developmental stage in question.[28] They are normal and legitimate developmental needs, and it is only their fulfilment – not their mere expression[29] – that can transmute and alter the grandiose self, i.e. increase structuralization and further the developmental process. This structuralization has not yet taken place, and so it is somewhat misleading to speak of integrating the grandiose self into the 'adult personality'[30] or into the 'structure of the reality ego',[31] since the latter do not yet exist. Their very existence depends on the structuralization that has yet to take place. Prior to such structuralization, what we find are essentially the autonomous ego-functions and the narcissistic structures of the inchoate ego.

It is not adequate to state that lack of self-esteem is due to the fact that 'a great deal of the narcissistic libido has remained concentrated upon the submerged archaic structure'.[32] Lack of self-esteem is simply a corollary of incomplete intrapsychic development, i.e. there is little self to be esteemed, and hence a selfobject is required for narcissistic homeostasis. In addition, it is not the concentration of narcissistic libido, but the lack of fulfilment of selfobject attachment-needs, that is involved in narcissistic disorders. Thus, 'transformations in the narcissistic realm' cannot depend on the 'gradual acceptance of the deep narcissistic demands by the reality ego'.[33] It is the *fulfilment* of narcissistic demands – by the *selfobject* – that results in the increased structuralization of the ego.

The remobilization of the grandiose self may take place in any one of the three forms of mirror transference: the merger transference, the twinship or alter-ego transference, and the mirror transference proper.[34] These distinct types of transference reflect the somewhat different demands made by the grandiose self upon the selfobject. They are to be classified according to developmental or genetic-dynamic considerations.[35] The specific type is determined by the pathognomonic fixation point.[36] In the mirror transference proper, the analyst is regarded as a separate person.[37] Kohut regards the pure mirror transference as closer to a developmental phase than the merger or twinship, and yet not even the former is considered a direct replica of a normal developmental phase.[38] I have already stated that I do not believe that Kohut offers adequate evidence of intensification or distortion. In addition, I would not wish to contrast the mirror transferences and idealizing transferences quite as sharply as Kohut does. He insists that the structure mobilized in each type of transference is 'quite dissimilar',[39] though even here he qualifies this by allowing that differentiation is often difficult, since both are narcissistic.[40] However, if the need for a selfobject is a function of incomplete structuralization (as Kohut himself asserts[41]), it seems a mere difference of emphasis in the form of the transference. In the mirror transferences, the emphasis rests more on the incomplete ego (which requires merger, etc). In the idealizing transferences, the emphasis rests on the needed selfobject (as required by the incomplete ego). But the two are entirely complementary. I would therefore agree with Kohut that the merger transference is an 'experience of the grandiose self'[42] – or, better, an experience of the *need* of the grandiose self – but I would not deny that such merger is sought with the idealized object.[43]

Kohut does in fact concede that 'the creation of the idealized selfobject and of the grandiose self are two facets of the same developmental phase . . . they occur simultaneously'.[44] I accept this complementarity, since it seems to be the corollary of Kohut's data as a whole.

When selfobject transferences arise, Kohut – illogically – insists on the nongratification of the needs involved.[45] The therapist is to acknowledge that their childhood precursors were appropriate – that these were more or less normal childhood needs[46] – but he is to prevent the satisfaction of these childhood wishes on an infantile level.[47] This policy of analytic abstinence and 'optimal frustration' seems utterly illogical for the type of problem under consideration. If – as we have argued – legitimate developmental needs are involved, acknowledgement alone cannot be enough. Developmental needs can only be met on the appropriate developmental level (even if this is an infantile level). Repression was significant only as a barrier to the fulfilment of attachment-needs, and it is the interrupted id-object link that is to be restored if structuralization is to continue. If – as Kohut states – the demands of the grandiose self are phase-appropriate,[48] let us take this seriously and meet these demands. Where development has been checked, a need that is forced to persist unmet is still as phase-appropriate in adult years as it ever was in actual childhood years. It is not chronological age, but the actual stage of development reached – whether or not in synchrony with the optimal developmental timetable – that determines what is phase-appropriate.

Kohut differentiates the biological *condition* of dependence and the psychological *wish* to be dependent.[49] This distinction does not do justice to Kohut's own data. It is not merely a wish, but a psychological *condition* of dependence that is involved where structuralization is incomplete. The correlative need for a selfobject – for a dependent object-libidinal attachment – is not merely a wish but an accurate reflection of incomplete intrapsychic development. There are 'structural defects in the self, and . . . selfobject transferences . . . establish themselves on the basis of these defects'.[50] An archaic condition *is* reinstated;[51] a developmental point *is* reactivated;[52] and thus interrupted growth may continue.[53]

The spontaneous reactivation of an early developmental stage takes place in selfobject transferences. Early conditions and needs not merely *can* be reinstated, but are thus regularly reinstated. The only decision that confronts the therapist is how to respond to these possibilities – to acknowledge such needs without meeting them, or actually to meet them and thereby to resume and further the developmental process. The potential for transference lies in 'pre-analytically established internal factors in the analysand's personality structure'.[54] As Freud insisted, transferences arise naturally, in all relationships. They are not *created* by the analytic situation.[55] This point is of vital importance, since it implies that the possibility of reactivation and reinstatement *does not depend on the therapist*. The potential for this arises spontaneously in the analysand, and the therapist can only help or hinder, by accepting the transference and taking its needs seriously, or by merely acknowledging these needs and yet leaving them unsatisfied.

It is unduly pessimistic to state, with Blanck and Blanck, that there is 'no direct pathway back to the infantile situation' (1974: 56). On the contrary, the infantile situation – of incomplete structuralization and the corresponding need for a selfobject – has persisted into adult years, *and is therefore immediately accessible*, as a contemporary fact. In principle, therefore, one should not discount the possibility of the 'direct correction of the failures of that period of life' (1974: 56). Early affront need not be 'irreparable' (1979: 90), and later repair need not be limited (1979: 11). I would suggest – on my reading of the preceding data – that the major limitation lies in the unwillingness of therapists to take seriously the reactivated need for a selfobject. The Blancks state that such needs are 'no longer age-appropriate' (1979: 100), thus confusing chronology with actual developmental progress. Contemporary objects are likely to disappoint (1979: 100) *only* because of their unwillingness to take seriously phase-appropriate needs in the developmentally affronted adult. It is not merely pessimistic but incorrect to say that 'the time is past, and one can no longer treat the adult as though development stopped at a certain point early in life and can now be resumed with the therapist in the role of a more benign parent' (1979: 123). The spontaneous activation of a selfobject transference indicates that the developmental opportunity is not past, but still very much present, and that it has an inherent capacity for resumption – provided that the selfobject is willing to cooperate. Therapists need not be 'baffled about how to provide a good symbiotic experience retroactively for an adult in compensation for past failure' (1974: 342). The means for providing such experience lie in the acceptance of the selfobject transference and the fulfilment of the attachment-needs involved.

The whole psychoanalytic understanding of narcissism requires revision. Kohut has made major contributions here, and I wish to suggest ways in which further conclusions may be drawn from his data, which go beyond his own conclusions in this area. Stolorow and Lachmann (1980) note the importance of defining narcissism functionally rather than economically. In terms of function, narcissism serves 'to maintain the cohesion, stability, and positive affective colouring of the self representation' (Stolorow and Lachmann 1980: 14–15). On the basis of the preceding discussion, a rewording of this definition may be suggested. Narcissism serves to 'promote further structuralisation'. There is little *existing* structural cohesiveness to be maintained, rather such cohesiveness is a goal to be worked toward. A *sense* of cohesiveness, in the absence of actual structuralization, is provided by the attachment to the selfobject. But this is not as yet the cohesiveness of actual intrapsychic structuralization, which is still relatively inchoate. Moreover, 'temporal stability' and 'positive affective colouring' are not separate and independent goals, but corollaries of the first and most central goal, of 'structural cohesiveness'. When structuralization has been completed, these will stem directly from the (intrapsychic) fact of structuralization. Prior to the completion of structuralization, such corollaries can only be mediated through the (external) attachment to the selfobject, as a substitute for psychic structure. Where there is neither structuralization nor selfobject, none of these desiderata can be present. The narcissistic object-relationship is not so much to maintain self-esteem (Stolorow and Lachmann 1980), as to build further the very structure of the self, on which all these qualities – self-esteem, temporal stability, positive affective colouring – are dependent.

Following Hartmann, Kohut speaks of narcissism as 'the cathexis of the self'.[56] I define narcissism as 'the cathexis of *objects* in the service of structuralizing the self'. This implies both agreement and disagreement with Kohut's formulations on narcissism and object-relations. He states that the assumption that object relations exclude narcissism is untrue. 'Some of the most intense narcissistic experiences relate to objects . . . in the service of the self. . . or . . . experienced as part of the self'.[57] I agree that the traditional antithesis of object relations and narcissism is incorrect. I would go further to state that *all*, not merely 'many', narcissistic experiences imply an intense object-need (selfobject need), as the direct correlate of the fact of incomplete structuralization. The only contrast to be drawn is between narcissistic personalities whose selfobject needs are being met, and those in whom such needs persist unfulfilled – whether through continued repression of the attachment-need, *or through the lack of cooperation of the selfobject*. The absence of an actual selfobject attachment must not be taken to imply the absence of such an attachment-need, since the latter is determined by intrapsychic factors.

Kohut further states that 'the antithesis to narcissism is not the object relation, but object love'.[58] The latter two are not to be confused.[59] There may be 'an intense object relation, despite the fact that the object is invested with narcissistic cathexes'.[60] Narcissism is to be defined 'not by the target of the instinctual investment . . . but by the nature or quality of the instinctual charge'.[61] These formulations do not seem entirely satisfactory. Having disposed of the traditional antithesis between narcissism and object-relations, it seems unfortunate – and unnecessary – to postulate a new antithesis, between narcissism and object-love. The data certainly suggest that we may differentiate between archaic (narcissistic) and mature forms of object-relations. But both imply love for the object, whether experienced as a selfobject or as an independent object. The capacity for *mature* object-love may be the ultimate goal (which in itself presupposes the fulfilment of needs for a selfobject), but mature object-love is not the only form of object-love. Moreover narcissistic cathexes *must* be cathexes of the object in the service of the self, since narcissism implies incomplete structuralization and a corresponding need for a selfobject. Prior to full structuralization, object relations *cannot* be other than selfobject relations, due to the state of intrapsychic need. Narcissism thus stems from, and is to be defined by, the level of intrapsychic development – which itself defines 'the quality of the instinctual charge'. Kohut states that 'the small child . . . invests other people with narcissistic cathexes, and thus experiences them narcissistically, i.e. as selfobjects'.[62] No other type of cathexis is possible for the small child – or, except superficially, for the developmentally affronted adult – since the capacity for object relations is a function of intrapsychic structuralization.

Thus, too, the process of maturation cannot be spoken of as the 'transformation of narcissistic into object-instinctual drives, i.e. as the shifting of drive aims from the self upon objects'.[63] Object-instinctual drives – attachment-needs – are present from the earliest times, and are of the essence of narcissism. Moreover, drive aims remain constant, as being the ongoing need for an attachment to an object. There is no shift 'from the self upon objects'. In the earliest years, the self is still inchoate, and the need for a selfobject – an auxiliary ego – is paramount. The earliest drive-aims are therefore for a selfobject, in the service of structuralizing the self. Drive-aims do *not* therefore focus on the self directly, but only on the structuralizing selfobject. And, as structuralization progresses, the object gradually functions less as a selfobject and becomes more an independent object.

Stolorow (1975) notes that the supposed antithesis between narcissism and object relations is 'an artifact of an outmoded economic concept of narcissism'. Despite his criticism of this antithesis, Kohut in effect rehabilitates it by his insistence on a 'separate line of development' for narcissism.[64] Why should we postulate a separate line of development? Narcissism merely implies a more archaic form of object-relations. Object-relations gradually become less narcissistic as intrapsychic structuralization proceeds. The data suggest a continuum, not a discontinuity. Kohut designates object love not as 'a change of the mobilised narcissism into object-love', but as 'a freeing of formerly repressed object-libido'.[65] This formulation in effect disregards Kohut's own evidence of incomplete structuralization, which implies that the capacity for mature object-love – which Kohut here refers to – has not yet been attained. Structural defects imply the need for a selfobject,[66] not an independent object. The only type of object-love that has been 'formerly repressed' is *archaic* object-love, the need for attachment to a selfobject. This *is* 'mobilised narcissism'. And, as this mobilized narcissism is gradually gratified, intrapsychic structuralization is gradually furthered and the need for a selfobject correspondingly diminishes.

Kohut reiterates the concept of separate developmental lines for narcissism and object love, as he outlines his major contrast between drive psychology and the psychology of the self. Within the framework of drive psychology, narcissism precedes and is to give way to object love. By contrast, the psychology of the self speaks of self/selfobject relationships, which serve as the precursors of psychological structures. By the process of transmuting internalization, these will lead to the consolidation of the self.[67] The two explanations do not seem to me to be mutually exclusive. Early forms of object-relations (narcissism or self/selfobject relationships) precede and are to give way to maturer forms of object-relations (Kohut's 'object love'), as a function of the process of internalization and structuralization.

It is the degree of structuralization of the self that regulates the capacity for object relations. Object choice is a function of identity; and the two are not to be contrasted or separated, since they are entirely correlative.

Thus, too, the overall contrast between drive psychology and the psychology of the self is unnecessary. The latter merely draws out certain unrealized implications of the former, and the two are to be closely correlated. This co-ordination of the two models may be spelled out in a variety of ways.

Kohut states that 'abnormalities of the drives and of the ego are the symptomatic consequences of [the] central defect in the self'.[68] On the basis of the preceding discussion, this would seem to be a reversal of cause and effect. It is the repression of the drive for attachment that blocks the process of structuralization and thereby results in the self remaining incomplete and defective. Drive fixations and correlated activities of the ego are not due to 'the feebleness of the self'.[69] Rather, such fixations *cause* this 'feebleness' or 'insecurity of the self'.

Moreover, it will be apparent by now that I have not found adequate reason to distinguish the ego (as traditionally understood) from the self (in Kohut's terminology). The data that Kohut provides for his psychology of the self seem to me to refer essentially to the structuralization of the ego, and do not require any additional postulate. While allowing that the term 'the self' can have a wider denotation, I believe that it may here be used largely interchangeably with the term 'the ego'. The ego is admittedly only one part of the threefold mental apparatus, but it is in a sense the focal point of the self, and its structuralization is crucial for the overall development of the personality. 'Self-pathology' should not therefore be contrasted with 'drive fixation and infantilism of the ego'.[70] Rather, self-pathology results from drive fixation and is to be equated with infantilism of the ego.

The 'core of disintegration anxiety' refers to 'the breakup of the self, not fear of the drive'.[71] This statement is correct, but it does not justify dichotomizing self-psychology and drive-psychology. It is precisely the protective repression of the drive (attachment-need) that blocks the normal process of structuralization. Disintegration anxiety thus marks an awareness of the incomplete self.

Similarly, drive experience is not to be 'subordinated' to the child's experience of the relation between the self and the selfobjects.[72] The child's drive experience here *is* his or her need for an attachment to a selfobject. Kohut concludes that the contrast he draws 'changes our evaluation of the significance of the libido theory . . . and . . . of some forms of psychopathology which classical theory viewed as being caused by the personality's fixation on, or regression to, this or that stage of instinct development'.[73] The evaluation of libido theory *is* changed – not by rejecting the concept of instinctual fixation, but by accepting the consequences of such fixation for intrapsychic structuralization. Narcissism involves the attempt 'to ward off . . . the loss of the archaic selfobject' or expresses the 'need for selfobjects in lieu of self-structure'.[74] But we do not need to conclude, on this account, that 'conflicts over drive aims . . . are secondary in narcissistic personality disorders'.[75] Conflicts over drive aims are primary in narcissism, in that the drive for attachment to a selfobject is repressed, and the need for such attachment thereby persists as still requiring fulfilment.

The conflicts presupposed in narcissistic disorders may be termed structural conflicts, in that the repressive function of the ego checks an id-impulse from fulfilment. Conflict is involved, but complete structures are not involved. It is the repressive function of the *inchoate* ego that acts to check the id-impulse. And, by checking the normal object-libidinal fulfilment of this impulse, the further structuralization of the ego itself is thereby checked. The pathology of structural conflict may sometimes be oedipal, but need not only be oedipal. Narcissism is itself a more radical form of pathology of structural conflict, where such pathology is *at the same time* a pathology of the self. Kohut affirms that the explanations of drive psychology, of the structural model of the mind, and of ego psychology are satisfactory for the psychology of conflict.[76] A psychology of conflict *is* at issue here, and what we are doing is to explore its implications for the structuralization of the self. A drive-defence-structural model of the mind is itself the bedrock of the psychology of the self, and itself requires and implies a model of the relation of the self to selfobjects. Guntrip regards it as 'hopeless to try to deal with ego-psychology in terms of instinct theory'. On the contrary, each is relatively meaningless without the other. The move 'from instinct-vicissitude to ego-development' must imply the development, not the superseding, of the former model (Guntrip 1968: 126, 123).

Pace Kohut, structure formation can and must be explained within the framework of object-instinctual drive psychology.[77] A focus on narcissism does not risk disregarding object-instinctual forces,[78] since such forces – the drives for attachment to selfobjects – are central to narcissism. Kohut asks how psychoanalysis has been able to use a drive-defence model without a psychology of the self.[79] The question is valid, but the answer should be the integration of the two. As it is, Kohut draws unnecessary antitheses, resulting in far too absolute a contrast between the two models. What Kohut's data suggest is a psychology of the self as a corollary to, and essential development of, the drive-defence model, which itself remains valid.

Kohut himself calls for further studies of the relations between self-pathology and structural pathology.[80] I believe that his own data suggest the way forward, towards increasing correlation of the two. The contrast he draws between the structural disorders of early psychoanalysis, and the contemporary focus on disorders of the self, is somewhat misleading. We have seen that drive-pathology and self-pathology are not to be thus contrasted. Conflict-solution and the establishment of self-cohesion[81] are both part of the therapeutic task in narcissism. However, there is a valid contrast to be drawn between the neuroses and the whole spectrum of more serious disorders. Classical theory *was* limited – but not solely by its focus on structural conflict and the structural neuroses.[82] The outstanding limitation of classical theory was – and is – its insistence on making normative a technique that has only limited validity. Interpretation *is* of value, but it cannot be the sole therapeutic instrument. Above all, it is utterly counter-therapeutic when interpretation is linked to the rule of absti-nence and non-gratification. Indeed, it is the rule of abstinence, rather than the value of interpretation *per se*, that I wish to dispute. Such a rule of non-gratification is totally mistaken when a legitimate and unfulfilled developmental need is at issue, viz. the need for attachment to a selfobject. The great leap forward will come when the need for selfobjects is taken entirely seriously *and fulfilled* – not while it continues to be reduced or dismissed by various qualifications. The logic of Bowlby's paradigm and of Kohut's data, as I have presented them, is to insist on the rehabilitation of the concept of corrective emotional experience.

4

Ego boundaries and the development of the ego

Further comments on the structuralization of the ego will be presented here: in particular, the relation of this process of structuralization to the development of boundaries between the ego and the id, and between the ego and the external world. This discussion will make use of Otto Kernberg's contributions, and will suggest ways in which I wish to criticize or further develop this material in the light of the preceding discussion and of the conclusions reached in *Psychogenesis* (Moberly 1983).

Kernberg criticizes Kohut for his neglect of aggression in narcissism.[1] He repeatedly insists on the need to consider aggression in narcissism and in the whole range of more serious psychopathology.[2] In speaking of the pathological predominance of pregenital, especially oral, aggression, Kernberg leaves open several options as to the possible determinants of such aggression: 'it is hard to evaluate to what extent this development represents a constitutionally determined strong aggressive drive, a constitutionally determined lack of anxiety tolerance in regard to aggressive impulses, or severe frustration in their first years of life'.[3]

In the light of my discussion in *Psychogenesis*, I wish to stress the importance of the third option mentioned by Kernberg, viz. severe early frustration – or rather, the occurrence of defensive detachment, in response to any event (above all, separation) that the child *experiences as* unduly stressful. This is a reminder that the stressful event that precipitates defensive detachment need not be a matter of deliberate hurtfulness by the parent – it may well be quite unintentional; and it may or may not seem exceptionally stressful to adult eyes (a point to be borne in mind when investigating the history of the patient). But the point is that, to the child in question, the event in question was sufficiently stressful to precipitate defensive detachment (following Bowlby's paradigm); and that this defensive manoeuvre was not resolved in childhood years; and that the normal developmental process of growth-through-attachment was thereby checked.

In the light of this, I would wish to criticize and rephrase certain of Kernberg's statements on aggression, in order to draw out a dimension of their significance which I believe that Kernberg – and much of traditional psychoanalysis – have not realized. I agree with Kernberg that aggression is important – but in what way is it important? Kernberg states, for instance, that the task of integrating contrasting self- and object-images (those libidinally determined and those aggressively determined) fails to a large extent in borderline patients, chiefly because of the pathological predominance of pregenital aggression.[4] I would suggest that pregenital aggression – or rather, defensive detachment – checks the task of integration only insofar as, and as a consequence of, the normal process of growth-through-attachment being checked (through the protective repression of the need for attachment). It is the ongoing attachment that – in the normal process of growth – facilitates the task of integration of such images. Thus, aggression does not itself check integration, but rather it checks the process through which such integration would normally be achieved. My criticism of Kernberg here is that he presents as a statement of direct causation something that I would suggest is in fact elliptical, linking two points that are indirectly related, and that need to be recognized as such. Similarly, Kernberg affirms that: 'The resulting lack of synthesis of contradictory self- and object-images interferes with the integration of the self-concept and with the establishment of object-constancy or "total" object relationships'.[5]

By contrast, I would affirm that it is the disruption in attachment that checks the integration of the self-concept, since the attachment is in itself structuralizing. Likewise, the repression of the attachment-need affects the establishment of object-constancy (here the statement is evidently tautologous). It is not the lack of synthesis of images that leads to these consequences, for such lack of synthesis is itself a consequence of disruption in attachment. This lack of synthesis may be regarded as merely an alternative statement of these problematic consequences. My criticism of Kernberg here is that his statement presents an effect as a cause, and that it is not in fact explanatory, as presented, but merely descriptive. Similarly, I question Kernberg's statement that 'the most important cause of failure in the borderline pathology is probably a quantitative predominance of negative introjections'.[6] While he allows that this excess of negative introjections may stem from severe early frustrations, his statement nevertheless seems misleadingly worded. Excessive negative introjections are an effect, not a cause. Again, Kernberg affirms that pathological narcissism is characterized by 'a pathological self structure which has defensive functions against underlying conflicts involving both love and aggression'.[7] On our present perspective, this self structure is in no way a defence against conflict, but simply a result of conflict. Both love (the attachment-need) and aggression (defensive detachment) are involved, but the checking of the normal process of intrapsychic structuralization – a pathological self structure – is a *result* of defensive detachment.

With Kernberg, I wish to stress the importance of conflict

and aggression in the etiology of serious psychopathology. With Kohut, I wish to stress the importance of developmental arrest in these disorders. However, I would see the latter as linked with the former: incomplete structuralization is a consequence of the protective repression of the attachment-need. Kernberg states that the main effect of aggression in the psychoses is a regressive refusion of self and object images.[8] By contrast, in borderline personality organization the chief effect is not refusion, but an intensification and pathological fixation of splitting processes.[9] I would wish to reshape these statements. In the psychoses, defensive detachment has checked the developmental process, *at a point at which* self and object images are still fused. In the borderline states, the developmental process has proceeded somewhat further before defensive detachment takes place. In both instances, it is the disruption in attachment that is of crucial significance. Correspondingly, it is not merely the resolution of conflict, but only the actual restoration of attachment, that can resume the process of intrapsychic structuralization.

Kernberg regards splitting as the defence characteristic of borderline personality organization,[10] and he considers repression to be a later and higher-level defence.[11] With Freud,[12] I have insisted that repression is the 'most primitive' form of defence. I see repression of the child's attachment-need as the crucial factor in the etiology of both the psychoses and the borderline states. Tentatively, I would also suggest that splitting may not be essentially a separate form of defence, but merely a description of an effect of early repression, when it takes place at a certain point in the developmental process. I do not regard splitting as a defence set up to protect the ego against unbearable conflict,[13] but as an effect of defence – or rather, as an effect of blocking the developmental process through repression. Splitting does not weaken the capacity for repression,[14] but is an effect of the successful use of this capacity. It is not 'excessive splitting' that inhibits the development of the ego core,[15] but the repression of the need for a structuralizing attachment. Similarly – and most crucially – it is not splitting that leads to a 'chronic overdependence on external objects'.[16] Splitting is merely an effect of the repression of the attachment-need. And, precisely because it is the attachment-need that has been repressed, this need remains unfulfilled and still requires to be fulfilled. In other words, there is naturally a persistent great need for dependence on external objects, which is developmentally valid and realistic. This need is in no way puzzling, since it is exactly correlative to the statement of what constitutes the problem in the first place, i.e. repression of the normal developmental need for attachment (dependence).

If Freud's view of repression as the most primitive form of defence is reaffirmed, several corollaries may be outlined. First, that one can and must speak of repression when the ego is still merged with the id. The capacity for repression of the attachment-need, i.e. for defensive detachment from the object, is to be correlated with the actual capacity for attachment to the object. Such attachment not merely predates the structuralization of the ego, but is itself the very means by which such structuralization is achieved – and without which such structuralization cannot be achieved. Repression of the attachment-need cannot possibly 'consolidate and protect the core of the ego'.[17] On the contrary, such repression checks the very process by which structuralization of the ego takes place. Similarly, repression does not 'contribute crucially to the delimitation of ego boundaries',[18] whether these are the ego's boundaries *vis-à-vis* the id or *vis-à-vis* the external world. By repressing the attachment to the object, attachment-needs thereby persist unfulfilled and still require to be fulfilled. Since there is, realistically, a persisting need for dependence on (attachment to) the external world, the boundaries of the ego cannot be delimited, since such delimitation is simply a corollary of the fulfilment of structuralization. The ego cannot be 'separate' from the external world until its needs for a structuralizing selfobject have been fulfilled.

Repression does not separate the id from the ego, but instead checks the process by which the ego is differentiated. The repression of an attachment-need – retaining it as an unfulfilled id-content – thereby prevents further structuralization of the ego, until such time as the id-object link is resumed. It is the structuralization of the ego that separates it from the id, i.e. such separation is an effect of the normal developmental process, not a consequence of defence. Van der Waals states that 'the repressed portion of the id is not pure id, but an ego id, just like the undifferentiated phase in the early part of psychic life' (1952: 68). Where the ego has not been differentiated and structuralized by the fulfilment of id-object attachment needs, one may well speak of repressed attachment-needs in terms of an 'ego id'. But I would hesitate to distinguish this from 'pure id'. Unfulfilled id-contents are, themselves, the potential from which the ego may be structuralized. Repression does not alter their character, but merely checks their fulfilment.

Kernberg states that a 'pathological failure of early ego development can occur because of a constitutional defect or retardation in the development of the apparatuses of primary autonomy which underlie the operation of introjection and identification processes'.[19] While not denying this possibility, I would not wish to ascribe it as much significance as Kernberg does. Kernberg affirms that 'perception and memory traces help to sort out the origin of stimuli and gradually differentiate self- and object- images'.[20] I would think that this overstates the point at issue. Perception and memory traces are important for the reception of stimuli, but it is the *evaluation* of these stimuli that is the crucial factor. When disidentification takes place (as discussed in *Psychogenesis*), this defensive manoeuvre does not impede the development or functioning of perception. But the object is considered so hurtful that the attachment-need is protectively repressed. The apparatuses of primary autonomy continue to function, but attachment-needs are no longer being met. The object continues to be perceived, but is no longer identified with, or depended on as a selfobject. Observational learning depends not so much on the capacity for observation as such, but most crucially on the willingness to identify with – or to receive the fulfilment of attachment-dependency needs from – the object that is observed:

'Indeed, when disidentification has occurred, the presence of same-sex models may only confirm the disidentificatory impulse. This is because they are no longer understood as models for likeness, but as models of what the person *cannot* be like, stemming from and reinforcing the aversive impulse.'

(Moberly 1983: 69)

Whether the object is of the same sex or of the opposite sex, it is the willingness for attachment, rather than the capacity for perception, that is of primary importance. Defensive detachment is not a cognitive-perceptive problem, but a volitional-affective problem – the refusal to be attached to the object that has been experienced as hurtful. Conversely, structuralization and identification are not *primarily* cognitive tasks, but most centrally involve and are dependent on the meeting of attachment-needs.

When the ego (or self) is still only inchoate, there is a need for a structuralizing attachment to the object as an auxiliary ego. The selfobject functions in place of structure, and an ongoing attachment to the selfobject is itself the medium for increasing intrapsychic structuralization. When the attachment-need is repressed, the process of structuralization is checked: the ego remains to a greater or lesser degree inchoate and unstructuralized, and there persists an exactly correlative need for attachment to a selfobject. The degree of this need for a selfobject marks, itself, the exact degree to which ego boundaries remain unconsolidated, i.e. the degree to which the inchoate ego still requires structuralizing support from the external world. Kernberg states:

'In the psychoses, there is a severe defect of the differentiation between self and object images, and regressive refusion of self and object images occurs in the form of primitive merging fantasies, with the *concomitant blurring of the ego boundaries in the area of differentiation between self and nonself.*'[21]

On our present perspective, such a statement must be regarded as purely tautologous. Lack of differentiation between self and object images implies refusion and merging (merging needs rather than merging fantasies). All three imply that the ego has not yet been sufficiently structuralized to be independent of the external world, but has a persisting need for a selfobject with which to fuse and merge. To speak of ego boundaries makes sense only where there is an actual structured ego, i.e. where a structure exists that can be 'bounded'. Differentiation between self and nonself is the goal of the developmental process – or rather, structuralization of the ego is the goal of the developmental process, and differentiation between self and nonself is simply a corollary of the achievement of such structuralization. Where ego boundaries are blurred, the process of structuralization is incomplete, and it is developmentally anachronistic to speak of possible differentiation between self and nonself. The self is still only partially existent, and the object necessarily is needed to function in the service of the self. The two items of comparison are not the self and nonself, but the inchoate self and the selfobject. One may even suggest that it is somewhat misleading to speak of the blurring of ego boundaries. It may be true that there is little or no boundary *between* the inchoate self and object. However, this does not imply that the boundary of the ego is blurred, rather that the boundary of the ego is still extended so that the object is still *within* – not outside – the boundary of the self. This is, after all, the significance and function of the selfobject within the developmental process.

On our present perspective, it is also in effect tautologous to state of the borderline patient: 'When self and object images are relatively well differentiated from each other, and when regressive refusion of these images is therefore relatively absent, then the differentiation of ego boundaries develops relatively undisturbed'.[22] These three clauses may be regarded as identical statements, not dependent on each other, but all dependent on the fulfilment of attachment-needs, which has taken place to a greater degree (prior to defensive detachment) in the borderline than in the psychotic. Likewise, as regards the psychotic, the blurring of limits between self- and object-images itself implies the loss of – or rather, absence of – ego-boundaries. The two are not separate manoeuvres, one 'subsequent' to the other.[23] It is not the lack of differentiation of self- and object-images that 'interferes' with the definition of ego-boundaries.[24] The latter does not 'depend' on the former,[25] but is merely an alternative statement of the same fact. Both depend on, and are to be correlated with, the fulfilment – or lack of fulfilment – of the needs for attachment to a selfobject. When Kernberg speaks of 'an environment sufficiently gratifying to prevent excessive refusion of self- and object-representations',[26] I would again treat this as elliptical – a statement of indirect causation that omits explicit mention of the central and most crucial factor. The environment is to be sufficiently gratifying so as not to result in protective repression of the attachment-need. It is defensive detachment that checks the developmental process at whatever point it may have reached, i.e. at some point at which self- and object-representations are still to some degree fused.

Kernberg's material includes much discussion of Jacobson's formulations. Following Jacobson (1965), Kernberg speaks of an originally undifferentiated self-object representation, out of which gradually develop the separate representations of self and objects. This fused intrapsychic structure implies that libidinal investment in the self and in objects was originally one process, and thus narcissism and object investment may be considered to develop simultaneously.[27] I wish to endorse this position, and to stress the importance of taking seriously its implications for the fulfilment of the developmental need for attachment. One may speak of an original, undifferentiated self-object representation, or – equally – speak of an inchoate self with a correspondingly massive need for a selfobject in lieu of structure. In the normal developmental process, the object originally functions only in the service of the not-yet-structuralized self. The object is necessarily a selfobject, i.e. it is undifferentiated from the self. For this reason, it begs the question to suggest that recognition of the mother marks the beginning of the delimitation of self and nonself, of self and external objects.[28] The mother is recognized precisely *as a selfobject*, as an extension of the self and in the service of the self – not as nonself. Similarly, frustration may well bring to awareness the painful absence of the fulfilling object, but it again begs the question to conclude that this contributes to the differentiation of self from nonself.[29] The absent object is the absent *self*object, and thus the experience may well be seen as an experience of the absence of part of the *self* (for this – on a developmental perspective – is a realistic statement of the function of the selfobject). Let therapists take note, since this also implies that the refusal to function as a selfobject is quite illogical on a developmental perspective and can only be counter-therapeutic. An incompletely structuralized self (as evidenced by lack of self and object differentiation, merger experiences, or the demand for a selfobject) requires a renewed, structuralizing attachment to an object in the service of the self. Thus, through the fulfilment (gratification) of the developmental need for attachment, the incomplete self may be further structuralized. As structuralization increases, the need for a structuralizing attachment to the selfobject decreases. Conversely, the continuing degree of need for a selfobject is the measure of the degree of incomplete structuralization. The two are entirely correlative.

On this model, I suggest that the difference between the psychoses and the borderline states is essentially one of degree, rather than of kind. Repression of the attachment-need checks the structuralization of the ego. The earlier this takes place, the greater the lack of structuralization of the ego. I would regard psychosis as radically incomplete growth, and the borderline states as relatively less radically incomplete growth. (Hostility and other negative manifestations in both of these states may be ascribed to the manoeuvre of defensive detachment which checked the developmental process in the first place.) When Kernberg speaks of psychotic regression 'to a more primitive stage of symbiotic self-object fusion',[30] I would accept this as a statement of developmental incompletion – of radically incomplete growth, as just suggested. In the psychoses, one finds largely undifferentiated self- and object-images, regressive refusion, and the blurring or lack of ego-boundaries.[31] By con-trast, the borderline states present a better degree of differentia-tion between self-and object-images – sufficient differentiation to permit largely intact ego-boundaries.[32] Partial refusion of primitive self- and object-images may affect the stability of ego boundaries,[33] but regressive refusion or lack of differentiation are not predominant in the borderline.[34] Insofar as differentia-tion of self- and object-images, and the correlative formation of ego-boundaries, are functions of a structuralizing attachment, it is hardly surprising that the persisting need for attachment is greatest (regressive refusion or merging) where least structur-alization has taken place ('a severe lack of ego development'[35]).

Borderlines present relatively greater differentiation, but here too the lack of structuralization is considerable. This is evident in the typical manifestations of borderline pathology, in the readiness with which transference psychosis occurs in the treatment of borderlines,[36] and above all in Kohut's material on the selfobject transferences of the narcissistic personality (whether taken as distinct from the borderline, or simply as a better functioning borderline). In that a selfobject functions in lieu of structure, the longing for a selfobject stems from and makes manifest the fact of incomplete intrapsychic structur-alization. The formation of ego-boundaries, or differentiation of self- and object-representations, is not yet complete so long as the object is needed as a selfobject. And this process will not and cannot be completed unless and until a structuralizing attach-ment to a selfobject is resumed and continued until it has fulfilled its developmental purpose.

Again commenting on Jacobson's work, Kernberg has much to say about refusion of self- and object-images as a *defence*.[37] By contrast, our present model envisages this as a *consequence* of defence. Or, more specifically, the consequence of defence (repression) is the checking of structuralization *at the point at which* self- and object-images are still fused. The consequence of defence is not fusion (an already given fact of the developmental timetable), but the inability to proceed beyond fusion (unless and until a structuralizing attachment is restored). I therefore do not regard 'refusion' as 'defensive' or the 'earliest protection against painful experiences'.[38] Rather, fusion persists in the aftermath of defence against painful experiences, i.e. after protective repression of the attachment-need from the hurtful object. Bad and frustrating situations may result in repression; repression of the structuralizing attachment checks structuralization; and incomplete structuralization implies that self- and object-representations remain fused. Thus, refusion is not a defence against frustration, but an effect of arrested development, which is itself a consequence of defensive detachment in response to frustration. I would therefore disagree with Kernberg and Jacobson as regards the relation of refusion to conflict, in the course of early development: 'extremely severe frustrations in relationships with significant early objects may bring about a dangerous refusion of self and object images, a mechanism which allows the individual to escape the conflict between the need for the external object and the dread of it'.[39] Refusion does not permit escape from conflict. It is merely a statement of the developmental stage reached at the time at which conflict occurs such that development is checked. Defensive detachment implies escape from the hurtful object, but only at the price of retaining the individual in a state of conflict between his need for the object and his dread of it. This is, after all, the very meaning of defensive detachment.

This model emphasizes the significance of developmental arrest, stemming from successful defence, in the more serious forms of psychopathology. Psychotic regression and 'defensive refusion' of early self- and object-representations are treated as equivalent statements, both signifying the arrest of structuralization in the wake of defensive detachment from the self-object. Severe frustrations 'interfere with the development of ego boundaries',[40] only insofar as they check the fulfilment of the normal structuralizing attachment – not insofar as they 'determine excessive defensive refusion'.[41] Refusion and the blurring of ego boundaries are, again, seen as equivalent statements, both pertaining to incomplete growth. 'Ego-dissolution' is not a 'threatening primitive danger',[42] but – less emotively – an acknowledgement of radically incomplete struc-turalization. Similarly, the fusion experiences of the psychotic – where differentiation of self from nonself is absent – may be regarded as accurate statements of the arrest of intrapsychic structuralization at the stage at which the need for a selfobject in lieu of structure is still paramount. The typical oscillation between 'idealized, ecstatic merged states, and terrifying, aggressive merged states'[43] is to be readily understood as de-scriptive of defensive detachment: fear of the hurtful selfobject does not abolish the need for attachment, but means that this fear coexists along with this tremendous need persisting as still requiring fulfilment.

Kernberg speaks of the relation between intact ego bound-aries and the capacity for reality testing.[44] He affirms a constant relationship between the loss of reality testing and the develop-ment of transferences with fusion or merger phenomena, and a similar constant relationship between the maintenance of re-ality testing and the absence of merger phenomena in the development of the transference.[45] I accept what is connoted by these statements, but wish to redefine what is meant by reality testing. This may be linked with my comments, in Chapter 1, on the meaning of 'reality'. 'Reality testing' may be defined as the ability to differentiate internal experience from external perception, the intrapsychic from the interpersonal, the self from the nonself.[46] However, where intrapsychic structuraliza-tion is incomplete, by what right may the awareness of this fact be denoted unrealistic? The fact as such may be unfortunate, but the awareness of it is arguably entirely realistic, and must therefore be considered a valid expression of reality testing in its own right. As currently used, the phrase 'reality testing' side-steps the issue. It is in practice used to denote awareness of the achievement of developmental progress. But where such prog-ress has not in fact been achieved, it would be highly unrealistic to expect an awareness appropriate only to greater maturation. 'Maturation testing' – or some such phrase – might be a better term. 'Reality testing' – if the phrase is to be used accurately and logically – must be treated as correlative with the actual reality of the degree of intrapsychic structuralization achieved, which may or may not be extensive.

To my mind, therefore, it is inaccurate to speak of reality testing in terms of the patient's capacity 'to identify himself fully with the external reality represented by the patient-therapist relationship'.[47] If the patient manifests shortcomings in this sphere, there may well be a problem of incomplete maturation, but not – strictly speaking – a problem of reality testing. The patient's capacity may well be realistic in terms of his relative lack of intrapsychic structuralization. I wish to emphasize here that I am not attempting to minimize the therapeutic problem involved. There is indeed a major problem, but no problem is aided by incorrect conceptualization. Similarly, I feel reservations about conceptualization in speaking of 'helping the patient to differentiate his internal life from the therapist's psychological reality'.[48] I accept the problem at issue, but would point out that the patient's internal life is the *reality* of incomplete structuralization. The problem is not one of unreality versus reality, but of two different levels or manifestations of reality. The patient needs to achieve further intrapsychic structuralization. The therapist's 'psychological reality' *qua* therapist is to provide a structuralizing attachment – to take seriously the reality of incomplete structuralization and therefore to function as a selfobject in lieu of structure, until structuralization is complete.

The problem is one of maturation, not of realism or reality testing. The beginning delimitations of ego boundaries marks an increase in maturation; but it is unfortunate to speak of this as the beginning of reality testing,[49] since the awareness of absent or incomplete boundaries is entirely realistic to the earlier stages of the developmental process (whether or not these stages may be correlated with the normal developmental timetable). The therapeutic task does not, strictly speaking, involve 'sorting out reality from intrapsychic needs'.[50] Intrapsychic needs *are* part of reality, too, and they are to be tackled and met realistically in order that the level of mature reality may ultimately be reached. Disintegration of the ego does not 'interfere' with work on separating internal needs from 'reality perception'.[51] An incompletely structuralized ego itself implies a perception of reality appropriate to the degree of structuralization reached. The situation may be unfortunate, but it is not unrealistic. What interferes with the further differentiation of the intrapsychic and the external is the repression of the need for a structuralizing attachment, which itself implies that the ego must remain incomplete, i.e. the intrapsychic is still structurally dependent on the external, and is by definition not differentiated from it. Reality testing is indeed 'a general structural characteristic of the ego rather than . . . a specific ego function',[52] in the sense that it is correlative with the degree of intrapsychic structuralization – at every stage of such structuralization. An awareness of incomplete structuralization – where such be the case – is entirely as realistic as an awareness of greater structuralization.

Difficulties in differentiation of the self-concept and of objects need not be said to interfere with 'the differentiation of present from past object relationships'.[53] On our developmental perspective, it is realistic still to require a selfobject in the present, if the need for this was not fulfilled in the past. It is not chronology, but actual developmental progress – or lack of it – that is crucial. Kernberg and the mainstream of analysis would speak of the confusion of transference and reality, and the inability to differentiate the analyst from the transference object.[54] By contrast, I have spoken of legitimate and realistic transference needs, and of the importance of the analyst being willing to function as the kind of object that is required by the fact of incomplete structuralization. The inability to see the analyst as an object in his own right does not lead to the weakening of ego-boundaries,[55] but stems from it and is merely an alternative statement of its significance. Fusion or merger phenomena do not imply a lack of reality testing, but a realistic awareness of radically incomplete structuralization, and the persisting and realistic developmental need for a merger attachment with a selfobject. Lack of structuralization in the borderline is extensive, but not quite as radical as in the psychotic. However, there is still a 'chronic overdependence on external objects'[56] – or rather, a persisting great need for external objects, a need that is developmentally realistic. And there is the syndrome of identity diffusion, which again is a realistic statement of incomplete structuralization.

Merger phenomena in the psychotic, and great dependence on external objects in the borderline, are both presented as a persisting and realistic developmental need for a selfobject – a need differing in degree, rather than in kind, according to the degree of structuralization reached prior to repression of the attachment-need. A few comments may be made in connection with this model. First, that recathexis in schizophrenia is not, *pace* Freud (1911), to be linked with delusional phenomena, but with the need for merger, i.e. recathexis or a renewed attachment at the developmental level reached at the time of decathexis (defensive detachment). Second, that Kernberg is right in stressing the importance in narcissism of the vicissitudes of internalized object relations.[57] However, I should wish to link these with, and interpret them in terms of, realistic needs for a selfobject attachment – working through any manifestations of the defensive detachment and permitting and encouraging a renewed attachment-for-structuralization. Kohut's material is excellent for suggesting the precise nature of the selfobject attachment that is needed, according to the developmental level attained (the merger, twinship, and mirror transferences). But neither Kernberg nor Kohut reach the point of realizing that legitimate and realistic developmental needs are involved – needs that require to be fulfilled (gratified) through a selfobject attachment. It will only be when analysis takes attachment-needs seriously that it will be able to advance in the realms of more serious psychopathology.

5

Developmental arrest and the inherent reparative potential

In the more serious forms of psychopathology, it is important to recognize the significance of (a) developmental arrest; (b) the persistence of legitimate developmental needs, which have not yet been fulfilled (on the optimal developmental timetable) and still require to be fulfilled.

This is not a non-pathological model, nor a dichotomizing of developmental and pathological considerations. As in *Psychogenesis* (Moberly 1983), I speak of developmental arrest as the consequence of a successful defensive manoeuvre: protective repression of the attachment-need checks the process of intrapsychic structuralization that takes place through the medium of an attachment to a selfobject. This manoeuvre of defensive detachment is adaptive insofar as it seeks to protect the inchoate self from an object that is experienced as hurtful (whether or not wilfully hurtful). However, the consequences of this defensive manoeuvre – unless it is very rapidly resolved – are developmentally disastrous. Intrapsychic structuralization is checked, and cannot continue unless and until the structuralizing attachment to the selfobject is resumed, and maintained without further interruption. The persistence of defensive detachment must therefore be regarded as maladaptive, and the resolution of this repression of the attachment-need is a notable part of the therapeutic task. This is not, however, the overall goal of therapy. It should be stressed that – owing to the very nature of the problem – the major goal must be the restoration of a structuralizing attachment to a selfobject, in order to continue the normal developmental process.

I agree with Kernberg that it is important to take aggression into account. On my view, this aggression is the hostility or other negative affects towards the hurtful object, that are involved in defensive detachment. However, where Kernberg speaks of splitting, I speak of repression – repression of the attachment-need, i.e. defensive detachment. And I regard this defensive manoeuvre as central to the whole spectrum of more serious psychopathology, i.e. the psychoses (see *Psychogenesis*) as well as the borderline states and narcissistic disorders. Moreover, I subordinate the question of defence to the more major concern of developmental arrest and the need to resume the fulfilment of developmental needs. Kernberg's position is an excellent statement of a traditional psychoanalytic approach, but he does not contribute – or even feel the need to contribute – to these developmental concerns.

Kohut presents a developmental approach, and is highly innovative in this respect. With Kernberg, I believe that Kohut does not do justice to aggression. And, in more general terms, I have already indicated that a self-psychology does include a psychology of conflict. The traditional drive-defence-structural model is to be incorporated and expanded, not superseded, by a model of the self and its relation to the selfobject. Granted these reservations, I find much outstandingly valuable material in Kohut's developmental approach. However, I also believe that Kohut did not realize the implications of his data – above all, that the need for a selfobject is realistic and requires to be fulfilled (gratified), not merely acknowledged. It is these implications of developmental realism that I have attempted to draw out in this study.

Dependence is a central concept for this developmental approach. It is regarded positively, as being phase-appropriate. I do not speak of 'pathological dependency needs',[1] but of realistic developmental needs for attachment. I regard it as utterly incorrect to label a legitimate developmental need as a defence. In his study of the borderline adult, Masterson states that 'this acting out of the wish for reunion through dependent relationships becomes the first target of treatment' (1976: 165). On our present model, this position is both illogical and counter-therapeutic. While intrapsychic structuralization is incomplete, the person in question does have a persisting need for a dependent attachment. This is in no sense 'a defense of the pathologic ego' (Masterson 1976: 164; cf. 60, 63, 169, 177, 252). The incompletely structuralized ego seeks attachment (dependency, reunion) in order to resume the normal developmental process of structuralization. This is reparative, not defensive. It is developmentally appropriate, and is to be encouraged, certainly not thwarted. To interrupt this manoeuvre can only perpetuate the problem, and this cannot therefore be regarded as a legitimate therapeutic strategy.

Similarly, a 'parasitical object-relation' is not to be regarded as a 'defence against separation anxiety' (Rosenfeld 1971), but as a reparative attempt to resume the fulfilment of normal early developmental needs for attachment. 'Good mother addiction' is not a 'defence against the deep depression of the early deprivation of mother' (Guntrip 1968: 3), but again a reparative manoeuvre, in response to the early deprivation of mother. Defence and reparation are not to be confused, since the consequences of this misunderstanding will involve the misdirection of the whole therapeutic endeavour. At present, it would seem that the term 'defence' is too widely and loosely used. Presumably the culmination of this line of reasoning would be the suggestion that therapy is a 'defence' against pathology!

In his discussion of narcissism, Kohut speaks of the

grandiose self as a 'defensive structure', and of the idealized parent imago as a 'compensatory structure'.[2] I would not regard either of these structures as defensive or compensatory, but would see both as effects left in the wake of defensive detachment. More specifically, both are normal facets of the early developmental process – which process was checked by defensive detachment, so that it did not proceed beyond a certain point. The inchoate self greatly needs the love of a selfobject. 'Grandiosity' is no more than a somewhat emotive designation for this developmentally realistic need. Defence (repression) may check the fulfilment of this need, but this defensive manoeuvre does not thereby create a defensive structure – it merely leaves the normal sense of great neediness in a state of unfulfilment. To speak of an 'idealized parent imago' is again to indicate the normal high value of the selfobject for the inchoate self. Partial structuralization of the ego itself implies a correlatively high need of, and esteem for, the selfobject. This developmental fact seems to account sufficiently for the phenomenon of so-called 'idealization', without any need to postulate some degree of exaggeration in it. Rather, this is normal idealization (high esteem for the selfobject). It is not created by defensive detachment, but the fulfilment of its needs is checked by this manoeuvre. In other words, it is a normal developmental phenomenon, not a compensatory structure. Kernberg speaks of the compensatory function of the grandiose self. He regards it as compensating for the 'ego weakening effects of the primitive defensive organisation'.[3] By contrast, I would regard the grandiose self as precisely an expression of ego weakness and incomplete structuralization, not a compensation for it. The only thing that may be regarded as compensatory, or reparative, is a renewed selfobject attachment. In the absence of such an attachment, no reparation or compensation can possibly take place.

The co-existence of inferiority and grandiosity in the narcissistic and borderline disorders provides a paradox that is more apparent than real. Narcissistic personalities have a great need to be loved and admired by others, and Kernberg speaks of a

'curious apparent contradiction between a very inflated concept of themselves and an inordinate need for tribute from
others'.[4] So far from being contradictory, the two seem to be
almost identical statements. The 'inflated' self-concept asserts
the self's great need for love – a normal developmental need
that unfortunately was not met on the optimal developmental
timetable. The great need to *be* loved and esteemed is of course
matched by the statement that the self needs to *receive* such
esteem and love from others. Where defensive detachment has
taken place, the need persists unfulfilled. But the need as such is
neither 'inflated' nor 'inordinate', but merely the normally
intense need of the partially structuralized self, and as such the
need is developmentally realistic. In the borderline states,
grandiose trends may underlie feelings of inferiority.[5] Again,
there is no contradiction. The great need for love was not
fulfilled in the ordinary course of development, as a consequence of defensive detachment. Thus, the need itself persists
(grandiosity), together with the awareness of its lack of fulfilment (inferiority). *Psychogenesis* has already considered this
apparent paradox in connection with schizophrenia:

'The basic assertion of megalomania is the proposition: "I
must be of great worth". However, this assertion arises
precisely from the blocking of its means for fulfilment. The
assertion is one of unmet need, not of accomplished fact. . . .
Megalomania is thus the correlate of a severe inferiority
complex. It asserts, not "I *am* of worth", but "I *should be* of
worth", but *have not* in fact been granted this sense of worth.
The attainment of a sense of personal worth . . . is *mediated
through* his relationships with other people. Thus, disruption
of an infant's capacity for attachment to a love-source is
bound in turn to have pathological consequences for the
sense of self-worth.'   (Moberly 1983: 22–3)

Thus, the inferiority-grandiosity paradox is to be found
throughout the spectrum of more serious psychopathology, and
it is a readily explicable phenomenon. Moreover, it is a statement of the effect of developmental arrest: the needs involved

are not pathological *per se*, though their lack of fulfilment is most unfortunate.

Kernberg distinguishes pathological narcissism from the normal narcissism of small children.[6] Several of his comments may be considered, and qualified in the light of our present hypothesis. First, the grandiose fantasies of normal small children are considered to have 'by far a more realistic quality' than in the case of narcissistic personalities. This is assertion rather than argument, and in any case it begs the question. Is chronology or actual developmental progress the more significant criterion for what may be considered developmentally realistic?

Second, the small child's overreaction to criticism and his demands for attention coexist with love and the 'capacity to trust and depend upon significant objects'. The fact that this latter capacity is not found in the narcissistic patient is merely an acknowledgement of the fact that defensive detachment has taken place. The contrast is not between normal and pathological narcissism, but between narcissistic needs that are being fulfilled and those that have been rendered incapable of fulfilment, through defensive detachment. In both instances, the narcissistic needs are normal. What is pathological in the narcissistic adult are not his needs, but their lack of fulfilment, and the persistence of defensive detachment.

Third, Kernberg sees the demandingness of the child as 'related to real needs', while the demandingness of pathological narcissism is 'excessive' – which again begs the question – and it 'cannot ever be fulfilled'. On our present hypothesis, such needs can and indeed should be fulfilled, but they must be treated as valid and realistic if fulfilment is to take place. Merely to acknowledge a developmental need, without actually fulfilling (gratifying) it, ensures that such needs do remain unmet and thus the problem (of developmental incompletion) is perpetuated.

Fourth, the negative features of narcissistic patients, such as aloofness and contempt, are again explicable as consequences of defensive detachment. The contrast with the 'warm quality of the small child's self-centredness' implies only that the latter has not undergone defensive detachment. Indeed, Kernberg himself notes that, in the history of narcissistic patients, one finds a lack of normal warmth, and a certain destructiveness, from the age of two or three – which suggests that this was the point at which defensive detachment took place in these cases. Again, the contrast does not lie between normal and pathological narcissism. It lies between those children who do not undergo defensive detachment, or in whom it is rapidly resolved; and those children who do undergo this defensive manoeuvre, and in whom it persists unresolved, thereby checking the normal developmental process.

The narcissistic needs of the child, and of the developmentally affronted adult, are both normal, in the sense of being developmentally realistic. Chronology and developmental stages should ideally be synchronized and not dichotomized. On an optimal developmental timetable, the two are harmonized. However, in the unfortunate instances where developmental progress is checked and thereafter does not keep pace with chronology, the developmental needs involved are still valid and non-pathological. The sheer passage of time does not alter the character of these unfulfilled developmental needs. A repressed attachment-need is still a realistic developmental need, and it still requires fulfilment, through the medium of a restored attachment.

Dependence is a developmentally realistic concept. However, its use in the discussion of psychopathology may be somewhat ambivalent. To speak of a person as dependent may mean (a) that his dependency needs are actually being met; (b) that his stage of (incomplete) intrapsychic structuralization implies an inability to function independently. The latter statement is true *whether or not* dependency needs are being met. When dependency needs are being met, through a selfobject attachment, structuralization gradually increases and the correlative need for dependence on the selfobject gradually decreases. But when dependent-attachment needs are not being met, incomplete structuralization persists and with it the lack of capacity for independent functioning, i.e. the state of dependence. Incomplete structuralization implies the need for a selfobject in lieu of structure. Indeed, this is itself the very definition of dependence – the need of the incompletely structuralized self for a selfobject – a realistic and developmentally valid need. The paradox of psychological development is that independence is attained through the fulfilment of dependency needs. The capacity for independence is a function of intrapsychic structuralization. And intrapsychic structuralization takes place through the inchoate ego's ongoing attachment to a selfobject.

The two meanings of dependency – the incapacity for independent functioning, and the meeting of dependency needs – should of course coincide. The former requires the latter. However, it is the tragedy of defensive detachment that the two may no longer be co-ordinated. The person in a state of structural dependence no longer has his dependency needs met through a structuralizing attachment to a selfobject, and thus he cannot any longer proceed towards increasing independence. Defensive detachment implies an intrapsychic barrier to attachment. However, if a therapist refuses to function as a selfobject, this too is an effective means of checking the fulfilment of the need for a structuralizing attachment. The resolution of defensive detachment is almost pointless if it is then considered inappropriate to restore the very thing that defensive detachment originally blocked! Where attachment-needs are concerned, the undoing of repression must *not* be regarded as an end in itself, but only as a means towards the most vital and central goal, viz. the restoration of attachment.

Dependence is here used as a psychological concept, but in a way that contrasts with Kohut's understanding of the term. Kohut states that dependence has biological and psychological meanings: the former refers to the *condition* of dependence, and the latter to the *wish* to be dependent.[7] Here, however, psychological dependence is understood not as a mere wish, but as a developmental state (of incomplete structuralization) and a developmental need (the correlative need for a structuralizing attachment to a selfobject).

I would venture a further innovatory comment, to be stated briefly, but based on the data presented both here and in *Psychogenesis*. This suggestion is that the concept of separation-individuation is usually stated too absolutely. What is generally spoken of as separation-individuation is certainly a major developmental landmark, but on the basis of the present discussion I should prefer to speak of this as the *inauguration* of separation-individuation. To adduce a developmental argument, the attainment of separation-individuation is essentially the meaning of adulthood. The earliest years, latency, and adolescence, all imply some degree of continued dependence and in this sense a correlative lack of separation-individuation. I would think it unwise to restrict the term to the earliest years of life, crucial though they be, since philosophically this is misleading. The young child has not attained separation-individuation in any absolute sense, or he would by that very fact no longer have any need for parental care. Moreover, to adduce a defensive argument as well as a developmental argument, we may consider what actually happens when early defence takes place. Defensive detachment *is* separation in an absolute sense, and it is precisely this that *checks* the developmental process. Psychological separation during the early years of life is a developmental disaster – and indeed this only reinforces the developmental argument that the earliest years provide only the inauguration of a process that must continue for a number of years thereafter. Borderline states are not, *pace* Mahler, Pine, and Bergmann (1975), due to difficulties in the rapprochement subphase of separation-individuation. They are due to the more absolute experience of separation that defensive detachment implies. True separation-individuation takes place within the matrix of the ongoing fulfilment of dependency needs through a dependent attachment to a self-object. This restates the affirmation that independence is met through the fulfilment of dependency needs, as a function of increasing structuralization taking place through a selfobject attachment.

In contrast to much understanding of developmental arrest,

this study presents a twofold model: developmental *arrest* as such, and the inherent *reparative* potential for resuming development. This latter point is particularly innovative, though at the same time it is presented as the logical corollary of the existing analytic data. Repression of a developmental need does not alter the character of the need – the need as such still persists, even though repressed. Checking the fulfilment of a need does not imply the elimination of that need. Repression of an attachment-need must be met, not merely by the undoing of repression, but by the actual restoration of attachment, i.e. the resumption of the process whereby further structuralization may be achieved. Selfobjects are required for intrapsychic structuralization, whether in ordinary development or in the therapeutic process, i.e. whether normal development takes place according to its optimal timetable or is resumed after interruption. Where psychopathology involves incomplete structuralization – in the functional psychoses, borderline states, and narcissistic personality disorders – the primary therapeutic function is, just as the primary parental function, to serve as an auxiliary ego or selfobject. The importance of the selfobject on a developmental perspective is outstanding, and advances in therapy must depend on taking seriously the requirements of developmental realism, i.e. meeting the valid and legitimate need for a selfobject, in lieu of structure and to promote further structuralization. Object choice is indeed a function of identity, not merely as regards gender identity, but more generally, in that the need for a selfobject is a function of incomplete structuralization.

The selfobject transference has both diagnostic value, as being indicative of incomplete structuralization, and therapeutic value, as itself being the means to promote further structuralization – *provided that* the therapist is willing to function as a selfobject, in order to meet these realistic developmental needs that have been transferred into the therapeutic situation. As Freud insisted,[8] transferences are not a function of the analytic situation, but arise spontaneously in relationships as a function of the individual's own relational capacity. I have added that transference includes realistic as well as unrealistic elements. Thus, to take Freud's point further, we may note that the therapist does not have to *create* the potential for developmental fulfilment, since this potential is evidently inherent and arises spontaneously in the form of a selfobject transference. The *only* question that faces the therapist is whether he will make use of and cooperate with this inherent reparative potential, or ignore or check it. The latter option is tantamount to confirmation of the problem. Yet merely to acknowledge the need for a selfobject, without fulfilling (gratifying) this need, implies a lack of cooperation with the natural reparative process. Standard analytic procedure does not do justice to the very nature of the problem, because it insists on retaining a model for technique that was originally shaped around a different kind of problem.

This study postulates an inherent reparative potential, through a renewed selfobject attachment (transference of developmental needs), in the more serious forms of psychopathology. This hypothesis also has implications for the concept of critical periods in the process of development. What happens during critical periods in the early growth of animals may well be decisive for further development and subsequently unalterable. For humans, this study suggests that there are no critical periods in an absolute sense. The earliest years are of crucial significance; but nothing negative that happens, or positive that fails to happen, is irrevocable *in principle*. The selfobject transference is the reinstatement of the formerly repressed attachment need. If this is accepted as realistic and legitimate, the developmental process of structuralization-through-attachment may be resumed. The needs of a particular period of early growth can still be met, *provided that the therapist is willing to accept and cooperate with the reinstatement of the conditions of that period*. This reinstatement of early conditions does not have to be *created* by the therapist. Intrapsychically, the situation and need of the patient are still as they were earlier on, viz. incomplete structuralization due to the repression of the need for attachment to a selfobject – a need that persists as still requiring fulfilment. If the therapist is willing to function as a selfobject – the only developmentally realistic therapeutic manoeuvre – further structuralization may take place.

A theory of developmental arrest based on repression – the repression of an attachment-need – is a dynamic theory. Arrest may be the consequence of repression, but the re-emergence and reinstatement of the repressed must also be taken into account, i.e. the renewal of attachment, through which further structuralization may be promoted. On this model, the very nature of developmental arrest, as being dynamically structured (the repression of the attachment-need) implies an inherent reparative potential (the emergence from repression and hence reinstatement and fulfilment of the attachment-need). When developmental progress has been detached from actual chronology, i.e. from fulfilment on the optimal developmental timetable, it may be resumed whenever phase-appropriate developmental conditions are reinstated. The nature of the therapeutic endeavour is spelled out by the nature of the transference (reanimation of developmental needs). The task of the therapist is to cooperate with this inherent reparative potential. He is to function as a selfobject, in lieu of structure and to promote further structuralization. The attachment-need, once checked, is now to be fulfilled. The solution is to be co-ordinated with the very nature of the problem.

The therapist is to function as a selfobject not merely initially or as a temporary measure, but on a long-term basis, on the understanding that this must be the central therapeutic strategy for problems of this nature. To begin fulfilling the need for a selfobject, and then to discontinue doing so, interrupts the solution and reinstates the problem. A selfobject attachment must be resumed *and continued*. Structuralization does not take place immediately but through the medium of an ongoing attachment, over a period of time. In the ordinary course of development, a young child does not grow up overnight. Similarly, in the therapeutic situation a prolonged period of time may realistically be required to make good developmental deficits stemming from the earliest years. To suggest that gratification perpetuates the problem or tends to make it interminable is short-sighted. Gratification may not provide a speedy solution, but this is inherent in the very nature of the developmental process. The realistically gradual pace of the solution does not derogate from the validity of reinstating the fulfilment of developmental needs. On this perspective, 'adhesiveness of the libido' is not problematic. It does not mark a resistance to change, but merely affirms that a legitimate developmental need cannot be bypassed. Such a need will only be superseded when it has been fulfilled. Therapeutic pessimism regarding the more serious forms of psychopathology is more likely to be a function of therapeutic dogmatism than of difficulties inherent in the problem.

Above all, there is a need to modify classical psychoanalytic technique, which was in any case designed for a limited model and not for the whole range of psychopathology. This modification is called for by the implications of the actual psychoanalytic data. In particular, it is important to divorce interpretation from the rule of abstinence or non-gratification. Interpretation continues to be a valuable tool of treatment, though the major focus in the more serious disorders must be the fulfilment of needs for a selfobject attachment. The rule of abstinence is to be rejected as utterly counter-therapeutic for such disorders, in the light of the data we have available on the importance of attachment-needs. The therapist's function as selfobject is vital for the treatment of all the more serious forms of psychopathology. This is to assert the positive value of gratification, as the fulfilment of developmental needs, as corrective emotional experience, and as a structuralizing attachment to a selfobject. Defensive detachment and all the negative consequences of arrested development are to be dealt with, but these must be regarded merely as steps towards the major goal of resuming a structuralizing attachment to a selfobject. Interpretation may well take place within this context – within the matrix of the ongoing fulfilment of developmental needs. This model does not advocate a purely supportive psychotherapy. Support is here understood as a structuralizing attachment to a selfobject.

It is regarded as the crucial factor for cases of incomplete intrapsychic structuralization, and it may be treated as the essential matrix for other therapeutic work.

Concepts of psychopathology must be matched by revised concepts of technique. It is important to do justice to the implications of the data, and not to insist that one model of technique must be treated as normative for problems it was never designed to fit. The logic of Bowlby's paradigm, of Kohut's data, and of my own work – both here and in *Psychogenesis* – is to rehabilitate the concept of corrective emotional experience. The future of psychoanalysis must lie in its acceptance or rejection of these proposed modifications.

Notes

SE = *The Standard Edition of the Complete Psychological Works of Sigmund Freud.*

Chapter One

1 Freud, S. (1896) Further remarks on the neuro-psychoses of defence. *SE* III: 162.
2 Freud, S. (1924[1923]) Neurosis and psychosis. *SE* XIX: 150. (1939[1934–38]) Moses and monotheism. *SE* XXIII: 127. (1940[1938]) An outline of psycho-analysis. *SE* XXIII: 203.
3 Freud, S. (1926[1925]) Inhibitions, symptoms and anxiety. *SE* XX: 105.
4 Freud, S. (1925[1924]) An autobiographical study. *SE* XX: 30.
5 Freud, S. (1940[1938]) An outline of psycho-analysis. *SE* XXIII: 178.
6 Freud, S. (1926[1925]) Inhibitions, symptoms and anxiety. *SE* XX: 153.
7 Freud, S. (1915) Repression. *SE* XIV: 146.
8 Freud, S. (1917[1916–17]) Introductory lectures on psycho-analysis, III. *SE* XVI: 410.

(1926[1925]) Inhibitions, symptoms and anxiety. *SE* XX: 92, 145.

(1940[1938]) An outline of psycho-analysis. *SE* XXIII: 185.

9 Freud, S. (1915) Repression. *SE* XIV: 146.

10 Freud, S. (1910[1909]) Five lectures on psycho-analysis. *SE* XI: 53.

11 Freud, S. (1925[1924]) An autobiographical study. *SE* XX: 30.

12 Freud, S. (1926) The question of lay analysis. *SE* XX: 203.

13 Freud, S. (1914) Remembering, repeating and working-through. *SE* XII: 152.

14 Freud, S. (1917[1916–17]) Introductory lectures on psycho-analysis, III. *SE* XVI: 455. My emphasis.

15 Freud, S. (1937) Analysis terminable and interminable. *SE* XXIII: 238.

16 Freud, S. (1926) The question of lay analysis. *SE* XX: 205.

17 Freud, S. (1925[1924]) An autobiographical study. *SE* XX: 30.

18 Freud, S. (1915) Repression. *SE* XIV: 149.

19 Freud, S. (1926[1925]) Inhibitions, symptoms and anxiety. *SE* XX: 157.

20 Freud, S. (1915) Repression. *SE* XIV: 151.
    (1926[1925]) Inhibitions, symptoms and anxiety. *SE* XX: 157.

21 Freud, S. (1920) Beyond the pleasure principle. *SE* XVIII: 42.

22 Freud, S. (1920) *SE* XVIII: 42.

23 Freud, S. (1920) *SE* XVIII: 18.

24 Freud, S. (1920) *SE* XVIII: 20.

25 Freud, S. (1920) *SE* XVIII: 18.

26 Freud, S. (1914) Remembering, repeating and working-through. *SE* XII: 151.

27 Freud, S. (1920) Beyond the pleasure principle. *SE* XVIII: 20.

28 Freud, S. (1920) *SE* XVIII: 36.

29 Freud, S. (1912) The dynamics of transference. *SE* XII: 108.
    (1900) The interpretation of dreams. *SE* V: 577.

30 Freud, S. (1917[1916–17]) Introductory lectures on psycho-analysis, III. *SE* XVI: 342, 364.
    (1923[1922]) Two encyclopaedia articles. A. Psycho-analysis. *SE* XVIII: 246.

31 Freud, S. (1917[1916–17]) Introductory lectures on psycho-analysis, III. *SE* XVI: 364.

32 Freud, S. (1915) Thoughts for the times on war and death. *SE* XIV: 286.

33 Freud, S. (1940[1938]) An outline of psycho-analysis. *SE* XXIII: 151.
34 Freud, S. (1940[1938]) *SE* XXIII: 181.
35 Freud, S. (1940[1938]) *SE* XXIII: 181.
36 Freud, S. (1915) Instincts and their vicissitudes. *SE* XIV: 123.
37 Freud, S. (1917[1916–17]) Introductory lectures on psycho-analysis, III. *SE* XVI: 359.
38 Freud, S. (1917[1916–17]) *SE* XVI: 280.
39 Freud, S. (1917[1916–17]) *SE* XVI: 455.
40 Freud, S. (1917[1916–17]) *SE* XVI: 455.
41 Freud, S. (1915[1914]) Observations on transference-love. *SE* XII: 166.
42 Freud, S. (1915[1914]) *SE* XII: 166.
43 Freud, S. (1914) On narcissism: an introduction. *SE* XIV: 101.
44 Freud, S. (1937) Analysis terminable and interminable. *SE* XXIII: 229.
45 Freud, S. (1919[1918]) Lines of advance in psycho-analytic therapy. *SE* XVII: 164.
46 Freud, S. (1915[1914]) Observations on transference-love. *SE* XII: 165.
47 Freud, S. (1905[1901]) Fragment of an analysis of a case of hysteria. *SE* VII: 116.
48 Freud, S. (1905[1901]) *SE* VII: 116.
49 Freud, S. (1905[1901]) *SE* VII: 116.
50 Freud, S. (1905[1901]) *SE* VII: 116.
51 Freud, S. (1905[1901]) *SE* VII: 117.
52 Freud, S. (1914) Remembering, repeating and working-through. *SE* XII: 151, 154.
(1920) Beyond the pleasure principle. *SE* XVIII: 22.
53 Freud, S. (1905[1901]) Fragment of an analysis of a case of hysteria. *SE* VII: 116.
54 Freud, S. (1914) Remembering, repeating and working-through. *SE* XII: 154.
55 Freud, S. (1914) *SE* XII: 154.
56 Freud, S. (1924[1923]) Neurosis and psychosis. *SE* XIX: 149–50.
57 Freud, S. (1925[1924]) An autobiographical study. *SE* XX: 42.
58 Freud, S. (1917[1916–17]) Introductory lectures on psycho-analysis, III. *SE* XVI: 442.

59 Freud, S. (1915[1914]) Observations on transference-love. *SE* XII: 167–68.

60 Freud, S. (1925[1924]) An autobiographical study. *SE* XX: 43.

61 Freud, S. (1925[1924]) *SE* XX: 43.

62 Freud, S. (1905[1901]) Fragment of an analysis of a case of hysteria. *SE* VII: 117.

63 Freud, S. (1925[1924]) An autobiographical study. *SE* XX: 43.

64 Freud, S. (1912) The dynamics of transference. *SE* XII: 101.

65 Freud, S. (1912) *SE* XII: 107.

66 Freud, S. (1915[1914]) Observations on transference-love. *SE* XII: 168–69.

67 Freud, S. (1910[1909]) Five lectures on psycho-analysis. *SE* XI: 17.

68 Freud, S. (1912) The dynamics of transference. *SE* XII: 103.

69 Freud, S. (1924[1923]) Neurosis and psychosis. *SE* XIX: 150.
(1924) The loss of reality in neurosis and psychosis. *SE* XIX: 183.
(1926[1925]) Inhibitions, symptoms and anxiety. *SE* XX: 155.

70 Freud, S. (1926) The question of lay analysis. *SE* XX: 204.

71 Freud, S. (1924) The loss of reality in neurosis and psychosis. *SE* XIX: 187.
(1940[1938]) An outline of psycho-analysis. *SE* XXIII: 203.

72 Freud, S. (1926[1925]) Inhibitions, symptoms and anxiety. *SE* XX: 95.

73 Freud, S. (1926[1925]) *SE* XX: 95.

74 Freud, S. (1926[1925]) *SE* XX: 156.

75 Freud, S. (1927) Fetishism. *SE* XXI: 155.
(1924) The loss of reality in neurosis and psychosis. *SE* XIX: 183.

76 Freud, S. (1926[1925]) Inhibitions, symptoms and anxiety. *SE* XX: 146.

77 Freud, S. (1926[1925]) *SE* XX: 153.

78 Freud, S. (1926[1925]) *SE* XX: 156.

79 Freud, S. (1926[1925]) *SE* XX: 156.

80 Freud, S. (1940[1938]) An outline of psycho-analysis. *SE* XXIII: 163.

81 Freud, S. (1926) The question of lay analysis. *SE* XX: 198.

82 Freud, S. (1933[1932]) New introductory lectures on psycho-analysis. *SE* XXII: 75.

Notes 91

83 Freud, S. (1933[1932]) *SE* XXII: 93.
84 Freud, S. (1940[1938]) An outline of psycho-analysis. *SE* XXIII: 163.
85 Freud, S. (1940[1938]) *SE* XXIII: 145.
86 Freud, S. (1905) Three essays on the theory of sexuality. *SE* VII: 218.
(1940[1938]) An outline of psycho-analysis. *SE* XXIII: 150.
87 Freud, S. (1917) A difficulty in the path of psycho-analysis. *SE* XVII: 139.
(1940[1938]) An outline of psycho-analysis. *SE* XXIII: 150–51.
88 Freud, S. (1905) Three essays on the theory of sexuality. *SE* VII: 218.
89 Freud, S. (1923) The ego and the id. *SE* XIX: 46.
90 Freud, S. (1940[1938]) An outline of psycho-analysis. *SE* XXIII: 150.
91 Freud, S. (1917[1915]) A metapsychological supplement to the theory of dreams. *SE* XIV: 223.
92 Freud, S. (1923) The ego and the id. *SE* XIX: 29.
93 Freud, S. (1933[1932]) New introductory lectures on psycho-analysis. *SE* XXII: 63.
94 Freud, S. (1917[1915]) Mourning and melancholia. *SE* XIV: 249.
95 Freud, S. (1921) Group psychology and the analysis of the ego. *SE* XVIII: 107.
96 Freud, S. (1923) The ego and the id. *SE* XIX: 29.
97 Freud, S. (1923) *SE* XIX: 29.
98 Freud, S. (1915) Instincts and their vicissitudes. *SE* XIV: 118–19.
99 Freud, S. (1915) *SE* XIV: 118–19.
100 Freud, S. (1915) *SE* XIV: 122.

Chapter Two

1 Freud, S. (1915) The unconscious. *SE* XIV: 197.
(1917[1916–17]) Introductory lectures on psycho-analysis, III. *SE* XVI: 447.
(1923[1922]) Two encyclopaedia articles. A. Psycho-analysis. *SE* XVIII: 249.
2 Freud, S. (1917[1916–17]) Introductory lectures on psycho-analysis, III. *SE* XVI: 280.

3 Freud, S. (1933[1932]) New Introductory lectures on psychoanalysis. *SE* XXII: 80.
4 Kohut 1978, I: 164.
5 Kohut 1978, I: 347.
6 Freud, S. (1900) The interpretation of dreams. *SE* V: 562–64.
7 Kohut 1971: 197–99.
8 Kohut 1971: 197.
9 Kohut 1971: 199.
10 Kohut 1971: 197.
11 Kohut 1978, I: 163.
12 Kohut 1978, I: 163.
13 Kohut 1978, I: 163.
14 Kohut 1977: 229.
15 Kohut 1977: 2.
16 Kohut 1977: 104.
17 Kohut 1977: 137.
18 Kohut 1977: 281.
19 Kohut 1977: 95.
20 Kohut 1977: 284.
21 Kohut 1977: 171.
22 Kohut 1978, II: 556–57.
23 Kohut 1971: 143.
24 Kohut 1971: 143.
25 Freud, S. (1936) A disturbance of memory on the Acropolis. *SE* XXII: 245.
26 Kohut 1971: 24.
27 Kohut 1978, I: 162, 220.
28 Kohut 1977: 217.
29 Kohut 1978, I: 219.
30 Kohut 1977: 16.
31 Kohut 1977: 259.
32 Kohut 1971: 294.
33 Kohut 1971: 46.
34 Kohut 1978, II: 815.
35 Kohut 1978, I: 219.
36 Kohut 1978, II: 789.
37 Kohut 1978, I: 219.
38 Kohut 1978, I: 225.
39 Kohut 1977: 84.
40 Kohut 1978, I: 506.

41 Kohut 1971: 25.
42 Kohut 1977: 210.
43 Kohut 1971: 290.
44 Kohut 1971: 291.
45 Kohut 1971: 291.
46 Kohut 1977: 4, 32.
47 Kohut 1971: 197; 1978, II: 555.
48 Kohut 1978, I: 432.
49 Kohut 1971: 51.
50 Kohut 1971: 51, 83.
51 Kohut 1971: 100.
52 Kohut 1978, I: 432.
53 Kohut 1978, I: 481.
54 Kohut 1978, II: 869.
55 Kohut 1971: 172.
56 Kohut 1971: 106.
57 Kohut 1978, II: 558–59.
58 Kohut 1978, II: 555.
59 Kohut 1971: xiv; 1978, II: 554.
60 Kohut 1977: 16; 1978, I: 225.
61 Kohut 1978, II: 789.
62 Kohut 1977: 249.
63 Kohut 1978, II: 896.
64 Kohut 1971: 86.
65 Kohut 1971: 90.
66 Kohut 1977: 137, 158.
67 Kohut 1977: 169.

Chapter Three

 1 Kohut 1971: 28.
 2 Kohut 1971: 105, 122.
 3 Kohut 1971: 125.
 4 Kohut 1978, II: 557.
 5 Kohut 1978, II: 554–55.
 6 Kohut 1978, II: 557.
 7 Kohut 1978, II: 740.
 8 Kohut 1978, II: 555, 558.
 9 Kohut 1977: 249.
10 Kohut 1971: 124.

11 Kohut 1971: 124.
12 Kohut 1978, II: 558.
13 Kohut 1978, II: 558.
14 Kohut 1978, I: 492.
15 Kohut 1977: 81–2.
16 Kohut 1971: 83.
17 Kohut 1971: 83.
18 Kohut 1971: 83.
19 Kohut 1971: 51.
20 Kohut 1971: 28.
21 Kohut 1971: 84.
22 Kohut 1971: 84.
23 Kohut 1971: 3.
24 Kohut 1971: 3.
25 Kohut 1978, II: 560.
26 Kohut 1971: 152.
27 Kohut 1971: 28.
28 Kohut 1971: 176.
29 Kohut 1971: 176.
30 Kohut 1971: 27.
31 Kohut 1971: 176.
32 Kohut 1971: 241.
33 Kohut 1971: 186.
34 Kohut 1971: 114.
35 Kohut 1971: 105, 133.
36 Kohut 1971: 134.
37 Kohut 1971: 115–16.
38 Kohut 1971: 124–25.
39 Kohut 1971: 34.
40 Kohut 1971: 34.
41 Kohut 1977: 259.
42 Kohut 1971: 114.
43 Kohut 1971: 114.
44 Kohut 1971: 107.
45 Kohut 1978, II: 558.
46 Kohut 1978, II: 558–59.
47 Kohut 1971: 197.
48 Kohut 1971: 176.
49 Kohut 1978, I: 173.
50 Kohut 1977: 259.

51 Kohut 1971: 46.
52 Kohut 1978, II: 554.
53 Kohut 1978, II: 554–55.
54 Kohut 1977: 217.
55 Freud, S. (1905[1901]) Fragment of an analysis of a case of hysteria. *SE* VII: 117.
    (1910[1909]) Five lectures on psycho-analysis. *SE* XI: 51.
56 Kohut 1971: xiii.
57 Kohut 1971: xiv.
58 Kohut 1978, I: 429.
59 Kohut 1978, I: 498.
60 Kohut 1978, I: 498.
61 Kohut 1971: 26.
62 Kohut 1971: 26.
63 Kohut 1977: 41.
64 Kohut 1978, II: 556.
65 Kohut 1971: 297.
66 Kohut 1977: 259.
67 Kohut 1977: 83.
68 Kohut 1977: 82.
69 Kohut 1977: 81.
70 Kohut 1977: 125.
71 Kohut 1977: 104.
72 Kohut 1977: 80.
73 Kohut 1977: 80.
74 Kohut 1978, II: 557.
75 Kohut 1978, II: 556–57.
76 Kohut 1977: 74–5.
77 Kohut 1978, II: 869.
78 Kohut 1978, II: 621.
79 Kohut 1977: 95.
80 Kohut 1977: 142.
81 Kohut 1977: 281.
82 Kohut 1977: 229.

Chapter Four

 1 Kernberg 1975: 286, 341.
 2 Kernberg 1975: 28, 229, 265, 271, 326; 1976: 116, 149, 163; 1980: 4, 12, 107.

3 Kernberg 1975: 234.
4 Kernberg 1975: 162–63.
5 Kernberg 1975: 163.
6 Kernberg 1976: 48.
7 Kernberg 1976: 116.
8 Kernberg 1975: 27.
9 Kernberg 1975: 27.
10 Kernberg 1976: 65.
11 Kernberg 1975: 179; 1976: 45, 65.
12 Freud, S. (1936) A disturbance of memory on the Acropolis. *SE* XXII: 245.
13 Kernberg 1975: 165.
14 Kernberg 1976: 51.
15 Kernberg 1976: 51.
16 Kernberg 1980: 13.
17 Kernberg 1976: 45.
18 Kernberg 1976: 45.
19 Kernberg 1976: 48.
20 Kernberg 1976: 149.
21 Kernberg 1975: 27. Kernberg's emphasis.
22 Kernberg 1975: 28.
23 Kernberg 1975: 173.
24 Kernberg 1976: 50.
25 Kernberg 1976: 125.
26 Kernberg 1976: 125.
27 Kernberg 1976: 115–16, 125; 1980: 95–6.
28 Kernberg 1976: 66.
29 Kernberg 1975: 26.
30 Kernberg 1975: 177.
31 Kernberg 1975: 27, 39, 162; 1976: 149; 1980: 11–12.
32 Kernberg 1975: 28, 34, 39, 162, 164; 1976: 149; 1980: 12.
33 Kernberg 1975: 24–5.
34 Kernberg 1975: 27–8.
35 Kernberg 1975: 39.
36 Kernberg 1975: 175.
37 Kernberg 1975: 163, 230–31; 1976: 66, 125; 1980: 96.
38 Kernberg 1980: 96.
39 Kernberg 1975: 231.
40 Kernberg 1976: 66.
41 Kernberg 1976: 66.

42 Kernberg 1975: 173.
43 Kernberg 1980: 109; cf. 1976: 125; 1975: 177.
44 Kernberg 1975: 28.
45 Kernberg 1980: 10.
46 Kernberg 1975: 83, 123.
47 Kernberg 1975: 182.
48 Kernberg 1980: 109.
49 Kernberg 1976: 37.
50 Kernberg 1976: 260.
51 Kernberg 1976: 260.
52 Kernberg 1980: 15.
53 Kernberg 1975: 166.
54 Kernberg 1975: 166.
55 Kernberg 1975: 166–67.
56 Kernberg 1980: 13.
57 Kernberg 1975: 270.

Chapter Five

1 Kernberg 1975: 187.
2 Kohut 1978, I: 99.
3 Kernberg 1975: 269.
4 Kernberg 1975: 17, 227.
5 Kernberg 1975: 33.
6 Kernberg 1975: 272–73.
7 Kohut 1978, I: 25, 221–25.
8 Freud, S. (1905[1901]) Fragment of an analysis of a case of hysteria. *SE* VII: 117.
(1910[1909]) Five lectures on psycho-analysis. *SE* XI: 51.

Bibliography

Ackner, B. (1954) Depersonalization. *Journal of Mental Science* 100: 838–72.

Ainsworth, M. D. S. (1969) Object relations, dependency, and attachment: a theoretical review of the infant–mother relationship. *Child Development* 40: 969–1025.

Alexander, F. (1957) *Psychoanalysis and Psychotherapy*. London: George Allen and Unwin.

Alpert, A. (1959) Reversibility of pathological fixations associated with maternal deprivation in infancy. *Psychoanalytic Study of the Child* 14: 169–85.

Andreas-Salome, L. (1962) The dual orientation of narcissism. *Psychoanalytic Quarterly* 31: 1–30.

Apfelbaum, B. (1966) On ego psychology: a critique of the structural approach to psychoanalytic theory. *International Journal of Psycho-Analysis* 47: 451–75.

Arieti, S. (1974) *Interpretation of schizophrenia*. London: Crosby Lockwood Staples.

Arlow, J. A. (1963) Conflict, regression, and symptom formation. *International Journal of Psycho-Analysis* 44: 12–22.

——— (1971) The structural concept of psychotic regression. In P. Doucet, and C. Laurin (eds) *Problems of Psychosis*. Amsterdam: Excerpta Medica.

——— (1975) The structural hypothesis – theoretical considerations. *Psychoanalytic Quarterly* 44: 509–25.

Arlow, J. A. and Brenner, C. (1964) *Psychoanalytic Concepts and the Structural Theory*. New York International Universities Press.

——— (1969) The psychopathology of the psychoses: a proposed revision. *International Journal of Psycho-Analysis* 50: 5–14.

Aronson, G. (1977) Defence and deficit models: their influence on therapy of schizophrenia. *International Journal of Psycho-Analysis* 58: 11–16.

Atkin, S. (1975) Ego synthesis and cognition in a borderline case. *Psychoanalytic Quarterly* 44: 29–61.

Bak, R. (1939) Regression of ego-orientation and libido in schizophrenia. *International Journal of Psycho-Analysis* 20: 64–71.

Balint, M. (1949) Early developmental states of the ego. Primary object love. *International Journal of Psycho-Analysis* 30: 265–73.

——— (1960) Primary narcissism and primary love. *Psychoanalytic Quarterly* 29: 6–43.

——— (1979) *The Basic Fault*. London: Tavistock.

Benedek, T. (1937) Defense mechanisms and structure of the total personality. *Psychoanalytic Quarterly* 6: 96–118.

——— (1938) Adaptation to reality in early infancy. *Psychoanalytic Quarterly* 7: 200–15.

Berg, M. D. (1977) The externalizing transference. *International Journal of Psycho-Analysis* 58: 235–44.

Bibring, E. (1943) The conception of the repetition compulsion. *Psychoanalytic Quarterly* 12: 486–519.

——— (1947) The so-called English school of psychoanalysis. *Psychoanalytic Quarterly* 16: 69–93.

——— (1969) The development and problems of the theory of the instincts. *International Journal of Psycho-Analysis* 50: 293–308.

Bing, J. F., McLaughlin, F., and Marburg, R. (1959) The metapsychology of narcissism. *Psychoanalytic Study of the Child* 14: 9–28.

Blanck, G. (1966) Some technical implications of ego psychology. *International Journal of Psycho-Analysis* 47: 6–13.

Blanck, G. and Blanck, R. (1974) *Ego psychology*, I. New York: Columbia University Press.

———— (1977) The transference object and the real object. *International Journal of Psycho-Analysis* 58: 33–44.

———— (1979) *Ego psychology*, II. New York: Columbia University Press.

Blum, H. P. (ed.) (1980) *Psychoanalytic Explorations of Technique*. New York: International Universities Press.

Bowlby, J. (1953) Some pathological processes set in train by early mother–child separation. *Journal of Mental Science* 99: 265–72.

———— (1957) An ethological approach to research in child development. *British Journal of Medical Psychology* 30: 230–40.

———— (1958) The nature of the child's tie to his mother. *International Journal of Psycho-Analysis* 39: 350–73.

———— (1960) Grief and mourning in infancy and early childhood. *Psychoanalytic Study of the Child* 15: 9–52.

———— (1960) Separation anxiety. *International Journal of Psycho-Analysis* 41: 89–113.

———— (1961) Separation anxiety: a clinical review of the literature. *Journal of Child Psychology and Psychiatry* 1: 251–69.

———— (1963) Pathological mourning and childhood mourning. *Journal of the American Psychoanalytic Association* 11: 500–41.

———— (1969) *Attachment*. London: Hogarth.

———— (1973) *Separation, anxiety and anger*. London: Hogarth.

———— (1980) *Loss, sadness and depression*. London: Hogarth.

Bowlby, J., Robertson, J. and Rosenbluth, D. (1952). A two-year-old goes to hospital. *Psychoanalytic Study of the Child* 7: 82–94.

Bowlby, J., Ainsworth, M., Boston, M. and Rosenbluth, D. (1956) The effects of mother–child separation: a follow-up study. *British Journal of Medical Psychology* 29: 211–47.

Boyer, L. B. and Giovacchini, P. L. (1980) *Psychoanalytic Treatment of Schizophrenic, Borderline and Characterological Disorders*. New York: Jason Aronson.

Brodey, W. M. (1965) On the dynamics of narcissism. *Psychoanalytic Study of the Child* 20: 165–93.

Brody, E. B. (1960) Borderline state, character disorder, and psychotic manifestations – some conceptual formulations. *Psychiatry* 23: 75–80.

Bychowski, G. (1947) The preschizophrenic ego. *Psychoanalytic Quarterly* 16: 225–33.

Cancro, R., Fox, N. and Shapiro, L. E. (eds) (1974) *Strategic Intervention in Schizophrenia*. New York: Behavioral Publications.

Carr, A. T. (1974) Compulsive neurosis: a review of the literature. *Psychological Bulletin* 81: 311–18.

Curtis, H. C. (1980) The concept of therapeutic alliance: implications for the 'widening scope'. In H. P. Blum (ed.) *Psychoanalytic Explorations of Technique*. New York: International Universities Press.

Doucet, P. and Laurin, C. (eds) (1971) *Problems of Psychosis*. Amsterdam: Excerpta Medica.

Eisnitz, A. J. (1969) Narcissistic object choice, self representation. *International Journal of Psycho-Analysis* 50: 15–25.

Eissler, K. R. (1980) The effect of the structure of the ego on psychoanalytic technique. In H. P. Blum (ed.) *Psychoanalytic Explorations of Technique*. New York: International Universities Press.

Fairbairn, W. R. D. (1952) *Psychoanalytic Studies of the Personality*. London: Routledge & Kegan Paul.

────── (1963) Synopsis of an object-relations theory of the personality. *International Journal of Psycho-Analysis* 44: 224–25.

Federn, P. (1953) *Ego Psychology and the Psychoses*. London: Imago.

Fenichel, O. (1941) *Problems of Psychoanalytic Technique*. New York: The Psychoanalytic Quarterly, Inc.

────── (1945) *The Psychoanalytic Theory of Neurosis*. London: Routledge & Kegan Paul.

Fine, R. (1981) *The Psychoanalytic Vision*. New York: Free Press.

Fleming, J. and Altschul, S. (1963) Activation of mourning and growth by psycho-analysis. *International Journal of Psycho-Analysis* 44: 419–31.

────── (1972) Early object deprivation and transference phenomena: the working alliance. *Psychoanalytic Quarterly* 41: 23–49.

Frances, A., Sacks, M. and Aronoff, M. S. (1977) Depersonalization: a self-relations perspective. *International Journal of Psycho-Analysis*: 58: 325–31.

Freeman, T. (1959) Aspects of defence in neurosis and psychosis. *International Journal of Psycho-Analysis* 40: 199–212.

────── (1963) The concept of narcissism in schizophrenic states. *International Journal of Psycho-Analysis* 44: 293–303.

────── (1973) *A Psychoanalytic Study of the Psychoses*. New York: International Universities Press.

────── (1977) On Freud's theory of schizophrenia. *International Journal of Psycho-Analysis* 58: 383–88.

Freeman, T., Cameron, J. L. and McGhie, A. (1966) *Studies on Psychosis*. New York: International Universities Press.

French, T. M. (1937) Reality and the unconscious. *Psychoanalytic Quarterly* 6: 23–61.

———— (1937) Reality testing in dreams. *Psychoanalytic Quarterly* 6: 62–77.

———— (1938) Defense and synthesis in the function of the ego. *Psychoanalytic Quarterly* 7: 537–53.

Freud, A. (1937) *The Ego and the Mechanisms of Defence.* London: Hogarth.

———— (1966) *Normality and Pathology in Childhood.* London: Hogarth.

Freud, S. *The Standard Edition of the Complete Works of Sigmund Freud,* 24 vols. London: Hogarth and the Institute of Psycho-Analysis.

———— (1896) Further remarks on the neuro-psychoses of defence. *SE* III.

———— (1900) The interpretation of dreams. *SE* V.

———— (1905[1901]) Fragment of an analysis of a case of hysteria. *SE* VII.

———— (1905) Three essays on the theory of sexuality. *SE* VII.

———— (1910[1909]) Five lectures on psycho-analysis. *SE* XI.

———— (1911) Psycho-analytic notes on an autobiographical account of a case of paranoia (dementia paranoides). *SE* XII.

———— (1912) The dynamics of transference. *SE* XII.

———— (1914) Remembering, repeating and working-through. *SE* XII.

———— (1915[1914]) Observations on transference-love. *SE* XII.

———— (1914) On narcissism: an introduction. *SE* XIV.

———— (1915) Repression. *SE* XIV.

———— (1915) The unconscious. *SE* XIV.

———— (1915) Thoughts for the times on war and death. *SE* XIV.

———— (1915) Instincts and their vicissitudes. *SE* XIV.

———— (1917[1915]) A metapsychological supplement to the theory of dreams. *SE* XIV.

———— (1917[1915]) Mourning and melancholia. *SE* XIV.

———— (1917[1916–17]) Introductory lectures on psycho-analysis, III. *SE* XVI.

———— (1917) A difficulty in the path of psycho-analysis. *SE* XVII.

———— (1919[1918]) Lines of advance in psycho-analytic therapy. *SE* XVII.

———— (1920) Beyond the pleasure principle. *SE* XVIII.

———— (1921) Group psychology and the analysis of the ego. *SE* XVIII.

—— (1923[1922]) Two encyclopaedia articles. A. Psycho-analysis. *SE* XVIII.

—— (1923) The ego and the id. *SE* XIX.

—— (1924[1923]) Neurosis and psychosis. *SE* XIX.

—— (1924) The loss of reality in neurosis and psychosis. *SE* XIX.

—— (1925[1924]) An autobiographical study. *SE* XX.

—— (1926[1925]) Inhibitions, symptoms and anxiety. *SE* XX.

—— (1926) The question of lay analysis. *SE* XX.

—— (1927) Fetishism. *SE* XXI.

—— (1933[1932]) New introductory lectures on psycho-analysis. *SE* XXII.

—— (1936) A disturbance of memory on the Acropolis. *SE* XXII.

—— (1937) Analysis terminable and interminable. *SE* XXIII.

—— (1939[1934–38]) Moses and monotheism. *SE* XXIII.

—— (1940[1938]) An outline of psycho-analysis. *SE* XXIII.

Friedman, L. J. (1975) Current psychoanalytic object relations theory and its clinical implications. *International Journal of Psycho-Analysis* 56: 137–46.

Frijling-Schreuder, E. C. M. (1966) The adaptive use of regression. *International Journal of Psycho-Analysis* 47: 364–69.

Fromm-Reichmann, F. (1939) Transference problems in schizophrenics. In F. Fromm-Reichmann (1959) *Psychoanalysis and Psychotherapy*. Chicago: University of Chicago Press.

Gero, G. (1951) The concept of defense. *Psychoanalytic Quarterly* 20: 565–78.

—— (1962) Sadism, masochism, and aggression: their role in symptom-formation. *Psychoanalytic Quarterly* 31: 31–42.

Glover, E. (1932) A psycho-analytic approach to the classification of mental disorders. *Journal of Mental Science* 78: 819–42.

Goldberg, A. (ed.) (1978) *The Psychology of the Self*. New York: International Universities Press.

Gordon, A. (1926) Obsessions in their relation to psychoses. *American Journal of Psychiatry* 5: 647–59.

Greenson, R. R. (1965) The working alliance and the transference neurosis. *Psychoanalytic Quarterly* 34: 155–81.

Grinker, R. R. (1957) On identification. *International Journal of Psycho-Analysis* 38: 379–90.

Grinker, R. R., Werble, B. and Drye, R. C. (1968) *The Borderline Syndrome: A Behavioral Study of Ego-Functions*. New York: Basic Books.

Grotstein, J. S. (1977) The psychoanalytic concept of schizophrenia. *International Journal of Psycho-Analysis* 58: 403–52.

Grunberger, B. (1979) *Narcissism*. New York: International Universities Press.

Guntrip, H. (1961) *Personality Structure and Human Interaction*. London: Hogarth.

——— (1968) *Schizoid Phenomena, Object Relations and the Self*. London: Hogarth.

Haas, L. (1966). Transference outside the psycho-analytic situation. *International Journal of Psycho-Analysis* 47: 422–26.

Hartmann, H. (1958[1939]) *Ego Psychology and the Problem of Adaptation*. London: Imago.

——— (1950) Psychoanalysis and developmental psychology. *Psychoanalytic Study of the Child* 5: 7–17.

——— (1950) Comments on the psychoanalytic theory of the ego. *Psychoanalytic Study of the Child* 5: 74–96.

——— (1951) Technical implications of ego psychology. *Psychoanalytic Quarterly* 20: 31–43.

——— (1952) The mutual influences in the development of ego and id. *Psychoanalytic Study of the Child* 7: 9–30.

——— (1956) The development of the ego concept in Freud's work. *International Journal of Psycho-Analysis* 37: 425–38.

——— (1964) *Essays on Ego Psychology*. New York: International Universities Press.

Hartmann, H. and Kris, E. (1945) The genetic approach in psychoanalysis. *Psychoanalytic Study of the Child* 1: 11–30.

Hartmann, H., Kris, E. and Loewenstein, R. M. (1946) Comments on the formation of psychic structure. *Psychoanalytic Study of the Child* 2: 11–38.

——— (1949) Notes on the theory of aggression. *Psychoanalytic Study of the Child* 3/4: 9–36.

Hartocollis, P. (ed.) (1977) *Borderline Personality Disorders*. New York: International Universities Press.

Heimann, P. (1956) Dynamics of transference interpretations. *International Journal of Psycho-Analysis*, 37: 303–10.

Heinicke, C. M. and Westheimer, I. (1965) *Brief Separations*. New York. International Universities Press.

Hendrick, I. (1942) Instinct and the ego during infancy. *Psychoanalytic Quarterly* 11: 33–58.

———— (1951) Early development of the ego: identification in infancy. *Psychoanalytic Quarterly* 20: 44–61.

Hill, L. B. (1938) The use of hostility as defense. *Psychoanalytic Quarterly* 7: 254–64.

Hoffer, W. (1950) Oral aggressiveness and ego development. *International Journal of Psycho-Analysis*, 31: 156–60.

———— (1956) Transference and transference neurosis. *International Journal of Psycho-Analysis*, 37: 377–79.

———— (1968) Notes on the theory of defense. *Psychoanalytic Study of the Child* 23: 178–88.

Holt, R. R. (1975) The past and future of ego psychology. *Psychoanalytic Quarterly* 44: 550–76.

Jacobson, E. (1965) *The Self and the Object World*. London: Hogarth.

Johnson, A. M. (1953) Factors in the etiology of fixations and symptom choice. *Psychoanalytic Quarterly* 22: 475–96.

Joseph, E. D. (1975) Clinical formulations and research. *Psychoanalytic Quarterly* 44: 526–33.

Kahn, E. and Cohen, L. H. (1932) Conflict and integration in schizophrenic development. *American Journal of Psychiatry* 11: 1025 –34.

Kasanin, J. (1933) The acute schizoaffective psychoses. *American Journal of Psychiatry* 13: 97–126.

Kemali, D., Bartholini, G., and Richter, D. (eds) (1976) *Schizophrenia Today*. Oxford: Pergamon.

Kepecs, J. G. (1966) Theories of transference neurosis. *Psychoanalytic Quarterly* 35: 497–521.

Kernberg, O. (1966) Structural derivatives of object relationships. *International Journal of Psycho-Analysis* 47: 236–53.

———— (1969) A contribution to the ego-psychological critique of the Kleinian school. *International Journal of Psycho-Analysis* 50: 317–33.

———— (1975) *Borderline Conditions and Pathological Narcissism*. New York: Jason Aronson.

———— (1976) *Object Relations Theory and Clinical Psychoanalysis*. New York: Jason Aronson.

———— (1980) *Internal World and External Reality*. New York: Jason Aronson.

Khan, M. M. R. (1974) *The Privacy of the Self*. London: Hogarth.

Klein, M. (1952) The origins of transference. *International Journal of Psycho-Analysis* 33: 433–38.

Kohut, H. (1971) *The Analysis of the Self.* New York: International Universities Press.
—— (1977) *The Restoration of the Self.* New York: International Universities Press.
—— (1978) *The Search for the Self,* I and II. Ed. P. H. Ornstein. New York: International Universities Press.
Krapf, E. E. (1956) Cold and warmth in the transference experience. *International Journal of Psycho-Analysis* 37: 389–91.
—— (1957) Transference and motility. *Psychoanalytic Quarterly* 26: 519–26.
Kris, E. (1950) Notes on the development and on some current problems of psychoanalytic child psychology. *Psychoanalytic Study of the Child* 5: 24–46.
Kubie, L. S. (1939) A critical analysis of the concept of a repetition compulsion. *International Journal of Psycho-Analysis* 20: 390–402.
—— (1941) The repetitive core of neurosis. *Psychoanalytic Quarterly* 10: 23–43.
Lampl-de Groot, J. (1956) The theory of instinctual drives. *International Journal of Psycho-Analysis* 37: 354–59.
Langs, R. (1976, 1978) *The Technique of Psychoanalytic Psychotherapy.* 2 vols. New York: Jason Aronson.
Laplanche, J. and Pontalis, J-B. (1980) *The Language of Psycho-Analysis.* London: Hogarth.
Leites, N. (1977) Transference interpretations *only? International Journal of Psycho-Analysis* 58: 275–87.
Levitan, H. L. (1969) The depersonalizing process. *Psychoanalytic Quarterly* 38: 97–109.
Lewis, N. D. C. and Blanchard, E. (1931) Clinical findings in 'recovered' cases of schizophrenia. *American Journal of Psychiatry* 11: 481–92.
Lichtenstein, H. (1964) The role of narcissism in the emergence and maintenance of a primary identity. *International Journal of Psycho-Analysis* 45: 49–56.
Lidz, T. (1975) *The Origin and Treatment of Schizophrenic Disorders.* London: Hutchinson.
Lipin, T. (1963) The repetition compulsion and 'maturational' drive-representatives. *International Journal of Psycho-Analysis* 44: 389–406.
Lipson, C. T. (1963) Denial and mourning. *International Journal of Psycho-Analysis* 44: 104–7.

Little, M. (1966) Transference in borderline states. *International Journal of Psycho-Analysis* 47: 476–85.

Loewald, H. W. (1962) Internalization, separation, mourning, and the superego. *Psychoanalytic Quarterly* 31: 483–504.

Loewenstein, R. M. (1969) Developments in the theory of transference in the last fifty years. *International Journal of Psycho-Analysis* 50: 583–88.

———— (1972) Ego autonomy and psychoanalytic technique. *Psychoanalytic Quarterly* 41: 1–22.

Macalpine, I. (1950) The development of the transference. *Psychoanalytic Quarterly* 19: 501–39.

Madison, P. (1956) Freud's repression concept. *International Journal of Psycho-Analysis* 37: 75–81.

Mahler, M. S. (1952) On child psychosis and schizophrenia. *Psychoanalytic Study of the Child* 7: 286–305.

———— (1968) *On Human Symbiosis and the Vicissitudes of Individuation.* New York: International Universities Press.

———— (1972) Rapprochement subphase of the separation-individuation process. *Psychoanalytic Quarterly* 41: 487–506.

Mahler, M. S. and Gosliner, B. J. (1955) On symbiotic child psychosis. *Psychoanalytic Study of the Child* 10: 195–212.

Mahler, M. S. and Furer, M. (1960) Observations on research regarding the 'symbiotic syndrome' of infantile psychosis. *Psychoanalytic Quarterly* 29: 317–27.

Mahler, M. S., Pine, F. and Bergmann, A. (1975) *The Psychological Birth of the Human Infant.* London: Hutchinson.

Malamud, W. and Render, N. (1939) Course and prognosis in schizophrenia. *American Journal of Psychiatry* 95: 1039–57.

Malev, M. (1969) Use of the repetition compulsion by the ego. *Psychoanalytic Quarterly* 38: 52–71.

Masterson, J. F. (1976) *Psychotherapy of the Borderline Adult.* New York: Brunner/Mazel.

Masterson, J. F. and Rinsley, D. B. (1975) The borderline syndrome: the role of the mother in the genesis and psychic structure of the borderline personality. *International Journal of Psycho-Analysis* 56: 163–77.

Meissner, W. W. (1970) Notes on identification. *Psychoanalytic Quarterly* 39: 563–89.

Menaker, E. (1953) Masochism – a defense reaction of the ego. *Psychoanalytic Quarterly* 22: 205–20.

Moberly, E. R. (1983) *Psychogenesis*. London: Routledge & Kegan Paul.

Modell, A. H. (1975) The ego and the id: fifty years later. *International Journal of Psycho-Analysis* 56: 57–68.

Myerson, A. (1936) Neuroses and neuropsychoses. *American Journal of Psychiatry* 93: 263–301.

Nacht, S. (1957) Technical remarks on the handling of the transference neurosis. *International Journal of Psycho-Analysis* 38: 196–203.

Needles, W. (1962) Eros and the repetition compulsion. *Psychoanalytic Quarterly* 31: 505–13.

Novey, S. (1960) The outpatient treatment of borderline paranoid states. *Psychiatry* 23: 357–64.

Nunberg, H. (1951) Transference and reality. *International Journal of Psycho-Analysis* 32: 1–9.

Orr, D. W. (1942) Is there a homeostatic instinct? *Psychoanalytic Quarterly* 11: 322–35.

Ostow, M. (1957) The erotic instincts – a contribution to the study of instincts. *International Journal of Psycho-Analysis* 38: 305–24.

Pao, P. (1977) On the formation of schizophrenic symptoms. *International Journal of Psycho-Analysis* 58: 389–401.

Peterfreund, E. (1975) The need for a new general theoretical frame of reference for psychoanalysis. *Psychoanalytic Quarterly* 44: 534–49.

Phillips, L. (1953) Case history data and prognosis in schizophrenia. *Journal of Nervous and Mental Disease* 117: 515–25.

Racker, H. (1954) Notes on the theory of transference. *Psychoanalytic Quarterly* 23: 78–86.

——— (1968) *Transference and Counter-Transference*. New York: International Universities Press.

Rosen, I. (1957) The clinical significance of obsessions in schizophrenia. *Journal of Mental Science* 103: 773–85.

Rosenfeld, H. A. (1965) *Psychotic States: A Psycho-Analytical Approach*. London: Hogarth.

——— (1969) On the treatment of psychotic states by psychoanalysis: an historical approach. *International Journal of Psycho-Analysis* 50: 615–31.

——— (1971) Contribution to the psychopathology of psychotic states. In P. Doucet and C. Laurin (eds) *Problems of Psychosis*. Amsterdam: Excerpta Medica.

Sandler, J. and Joffe, W. G. (1967) The tendency to persistence in psychological function and development. *Bulletin of the Menninger Clinic* 31: 257–71.

Sandler, J., Holder, A., Kawenoka, M., Kennedy, H. E. and Neurath, L. (1969) Notes on some theoretical and clinical aspects of transference. *International Journal of Psycho-Analysis* 50: 633–45.

Saul, L. J. (1962) The erotic transference. *Psychoanalytic Quarterly* 31: 54–61.

Saul, L. J. and Wenar, S. (1965) Early influences on development and disorders of personality. *Psychoanalytic Quarterly* 34: 327–89.

Scheflen, A. E. (1981) *Levels of Schizophrenia.* New York: Brunner/ Mazel.

Searles, H. F. (1963) Transference psychosis in the psychotherapy of chronic schizophrenia. *International Journal of Psycho-Analysis* 44: 249–81.

―――― (1965) *Collected Papers on Schizophrenia and Related Subjects.* London: Hogarth.

Sechehaye, M. A. (1956) The transference in symbolic realization. *International Journal of Psycho-Analysis* 37: 270–77.

Segal, H. (1956) Depression in the schizophrenic. *International Journal of Psycho-Analysis* 37: 339–43.

Siggins, L. D. (1966) Mourning: a critical survey of the literature. *International Journal of Psycho-Analysis* 47: 14–25.

Silbermann, I. (1957) Two types of preoedipal character disorders. *International Journal of Psycho-Analysis* 38: 350–58.

Silverberg, W. V. (1948) The concept of transference. *Psychoanalytic Quarterly* 17: 303–21.

Spitz, R. A. (1956) Transference: the analytical setting and its prototype. *International Journal of Psycho-Analysis* 37: 380–85.

Spotnitz, H. (1969) *Modern Psychoanalysis of the Schizophrenic Patient.* New York: Grune and Stratton.

―――― (1976) *Psychotherapy of Preoedipal Conditions.* New York: Jason Aronson.

Spruiell, V. (1975) Three strands of narcissism. *Psychoanalytic Quarterly* 44: 577–95.

Starr, P. H. (1954) Psychoses in children: their origin and structure. *Psychoanalytic Quarterly* 23: 544–65.

Stengel, E. (1945) A study on some clinical aspects of the relationship between obsessional neurosis and psychotic reaction types. *Journal of Mental Science* 91: 166–87.

Sterba, R. (1951) Character and resistance. *Psychoanalytic Quarterly* 20: 72–6.

———— (1953) Clinical and therapeutic aspects of character resistance. *Psychoanalytic Quarterly* 22: 1–20.

Stern, A. (1938) Psychoanalytic investigation of and therapy in the border line group of neuroses. *Psychoanalytic Quarterly* 7: 467–89.

———— (1948) Transference in borderline neuroses. *Psychoanalytic Quarterly* 17: 527–28.

Stern, M. M. (1957) The ego aspect of transference. *International Journal of Psycho-Analysis* 38: 146–57.

Stolorow, R. D. (1975) Toward a functional definition of narcissism. *International Journal of Psycho-Analysis* 56: 179–85.

Stolorow, R. D. and Lachmann, F. M. (1980) *Psychoanalysis of Developmental Arrests*. New York: International Universities Press.

Stone, M. H. (1980) *The Borderline Syndromes*. New York: McGraw-Hill.

Sullivan, H. S. (1931) The modified psychoanalytic treatment of schizophrenia. *American Journal of Psychiatry* 11: 519–40.

Szasz, T. S. (1963) The concept of transference. *International Journal of Psycho-Analysis* 44: 432–43.

Toman, W. (1956) Repetition and repetition compulsion. *International Journal of Psycho-Analysis* 37: 347–50.

Vaillant, G. E. (1962) Prediction of recovery in schizophrenia. *Journal of Nervous and Mental Disease* 135: 534–43.

Van der Waals, H. G. (1952) The mutual influences in the development of the ego and the id. *Psychoanalytic Study of the Child* 7: 66–8.

Weiland, I. H. (1966) Considerations on the development of symbiosis, symbiotic psychosis, and the nature of separation anxiety. *International Journal of Psycho-Analysis* 47: 1–5.

Winnicott, D. W. (1956) On transference. *International Journal of Psycho-Analysis* 37: 386–88.

———— (1965) *The Maturational Processes and the Facilitating Environment*. London: Hogarth.

Wolfenstein, M. (1966) How is mourning possible? *Psychoanalytic Study of the Child* 21: 93–123.

Wolstein, B. (1964) *Transference: Its Structure and Function in Psychoanalytic Therapy*. New York and London: Grune & Stratton.

Zetzel, E. R. (1956) Current concepts of transference. *International Journal of Psycho-Analysis* 37: 369–76.

Zilboorg, G. (1931) The deeper layers of schizophrenic psychoses. *American Journal of Psychiatry* 11: 493–511.

────── (1938) Some observations on the transformation of instincts. *Psychoanalytic Quarterly* 7: 1–24.

────── (1956) The problem of ambulatory schizophrenia. *American Journal of Psychiatry* 113: 519–25.

Name index

Subject index